The Best Canadian Poetry in English 2012

The Best Canadian Poetry in English 2012 2012

Guest Editor **Carmine Starnino**
Series Editor **Molly Peacock**

TIGHTROPE BOOKS
www.tightropebooks.com

Tightrope Books Inc.
167 Browning Trail
Barrie, Ontario
Canada L4N 5E7
www.tightropebooks.com

Editor: Carmine Starnino
Series Editor: Molly Peacock
Managing Editor: Carolina Smart
Copy Editor: Michael Groden
Cover Design: Deanna Janovski
Cover Art: Jessica Rae Gordon
Typesetting:David Bigham

Produced with the support of the Canada Council for the Arts and the Ontario Arts Council

Canada Council Conseil des Arts
for the Arts du Canada

ONTARIO ARTS COUNCIL
CONSEIL DES ARTS DE L'ONTARIO

A cataloguing record for this publication is available from Library and Archives Canada

Printed in Canada

Contents

Prologue

The Best Canadian Poetry in English 2012

Our fifth-anniversary edition of *The Best Canadian Poetry in English* arrives in exceptional style—and style is essential to poetry. In this art, style isn't merely fashion; it's an approach to fashioning. The flow of a poem can't exist without it.

Think of style as what energizes the relationship between form and content. In the anatomy of a poem, style is like the capillary action between the arteries of content and the veins of form. In practical terms it's the infinitesimal number of choices poets make as they choose words and decide on punctuation. In psychological terms it's the pattern of unconscious selections that draws a poet to a certain idea and allows a poet to exercise—or abandon—a certain structure.

Each year we ask another distinguished poet (with yet another style) to guest edit *The Best Canadian Poetry*. For our fifth volume we are honored to have Carmine Starnino as our Guest Editor. A poet of consequence and a fearless writer of his opinions on poetry, he brings to our series a capacious, varied view. With his eclectic taste, his finger on the pulse of younger poets as well as those with established reputations, and his zest for reading the hundreds of poems he perused to select the long list of one hundred and the short list of fifty poems for 2012, he poured through 54 print and on-line magazines. In his treasure hunt he found contemporary poetic Canadian style in abundance, and he describes it in his fascinating essay on our poetry today.

What were Canadian poets taking as their subjects in 2012? Here are some of their concerns:

anhingas, background noise, beaches, bears, Belfast, brothers, countertops, Don Draper, dreams, Evangeline, fathers, flowers, gallinules, gardens, Hamlet, herons, I, jars, killdeer, laundry tubs, loons, love, more love, microscopes, morning, mothers, a muslin dress, Northrop Frye, ospreys, a paperweight, parking lots, questions, rivers, ships, skinny dipping, stoves, swans, values, Walmart automotive, winter angst, winter ice, winter solstice, yearning, and a ziplock baggie of seahorse specimens.

Just collecting this list of nouns as a partial subject catalog gives us something of what comprises our 2012 selection—and that includes a glory of birds and water imagery everywhere. Yet careening down a list of subjects can't ever quite get at what our poets are thinking. A poem is only ever partly "about" something. In this, poetry defines itself against prose. A story may exist independently from its words (a tale can be told many ways), but a poem exists only in its words—and in the tangle of emotions those particular words evoke. That's why style is so important to poetry, and to this year's choices in particular. Its very ineffability makes poetry the anti-sound-bite.

Since 2008 (beginning with our inaugural Guest Editor, Stephanie Bolster, and continuing with A.F. Moritz, Lorna Crozier, and Priscila Uppal) we have selected 237 poets from 72 magazines for our anthologies. The yearly Bests can be found in high schools, libraries, university classrooms, hospitals—and carry-on luggage. Book clubs use it to try out poetry, lovers use it to find themselves, the curious use it for edification, and dreamers use it to translate internal landscapes. This project owes its life to the vision of Halli Villegas, publisher of Tightrope Books, a house that has distinguished itself by its upstart sass—and its own sophisticated style. An orchardful of gratitude goes to our cover artist, the stylish Jessica Rae Gordon, our designer Deanna Janovski, our managing editor, Carolina Smart, our publicist Nathaniel Moore, our vigilant proofreader Michael Groden, and our valiant designer David Bigham. I especially want to thank Carmine Starnino for his magnificent work and our stimulating phone conversations between Toronto and Montreal as we've discussed the conundrum of the Canadian Steam Punk Zone of prosody.

Our fifth-anniversary year also inaugurates Best Friends. Best Friends is a brand new eclectic (and dare I say stylish) group of supporters for The Best Canadian Poetry in English Series. Best Friends are poets, lovers of poetry—and lovers of poets. We'd be delighted to count you as a Best Friend, too. Please visit us at: www.tightropebooks. com.

Introduction

STEAM PUNK ZONE

In our mashup-mad era, we yearn for unpigeonholeability. We don't want to be different. We want to be weird. We want to be total category-killers. As a result, it's hard to find a poet—free-versifier and formalist alike—who doesn't believe at heart that he or she is far too heterodox to be trapped in existing definitions of traditional and experimental. Contemporary poetry now comprises a vast invented form: the godknowswhat.

That the selections in *Best Canadian Poetry in English 2012* echo and reprise this yearning should come as no surprise. From Rachel Lebowitz's unnerving, nursery rhyme-inflected prose cycle ("Cottonpolis") to Robert Earl Stewart's smoky, image-loaded stream of consciousness ("A Wind-Aided Fire"), this book is a mixed bag. It's the outcome, one might say, of a collective decision taken by Canadian poets to dart in all directions at once. To be sure, I plucked these poems from print and online journals with no bias except to find verse that provided a fresh entry into reality; that offered something, some equivalence between sound and feeling, I didn't already know, or couldn't find elsewhere. Good poets are stylists, and I hunted for styles whose distinctive qualities generated memorable insights. Yet, when assembled, many of the one-of-a-kind elements I admired—which each seemed unexpected, an emergency measure—turned out to share the same triggers. It made me uneasy. Don't misunderstand: these are wickedly good poems. But the task of finding them has forced me to reflect on the high price of writing under the influence of what F.R. Leavis would have called our "poetical modes."

On my desk, sit three squat anthologies from three countries: *Identity Parade* edited by Roddy Lumsden, published in the UK; *American Hybrid*, edited by David St. John and Cole Swenson, published in the US; and *Open Field* edited by Canadian Sina Queyras. All appeared within the last seven years. To read them, close on the heels of one another, is to be left agape at the current scale of Anglo-American verse. The books add up to 1200 pages, nearly one thousand poems and comprise almost two hundred poets from three countries (U.K., U.S. and Canadian, respectively). And that's only as far as these three tomes will let us see: there's a good deal more out there. One recalls Ian Hamilton's observation, back in 1994, that English poetry "can no longer be thought of in the singular." The shift, he argued, was from poetry to poetries. The fissioning has since escalated until, at present, English-language poets all seem to speak in tongues. Everywhere we're overrun by franchises of self-defined difference. To a certain extent, this is bardoltry as usual. Good poets have always tried to stand apart from their literary age. But today that individualism, to be accordingly recognized, needs to pay fealty to a period that has scrambled easy classifications. And what does such a period demand of our poems? Boundary-crossing, genre-splicing, exploratory flings between once-irreconcilable techniques. There may no longer be a generally endorsed sense of what constitutes poetry, but almost everyone agrees on what a poet needs to do in order not to be left behind. Thanks to the internet, even national identity is growing increasingly irrelevant as cultural trends continue to be erased by a global synching-up of motives. *Identity Parade* surveys the "pluralist" generation of British and Irish poetry, *American Hybrid* showcases U.S. models of "hybridization" and *Open Field* herds Canadians who reveal a "particular blend of formal and innovative work." English-speaking poets may be separated by a border and an ocean, but the zeitgeist has assigned each of us the same thesis.

Canadian poetry seems ideally suited to this era. Its masterworks, such as Irving Layton's "A Tall Man Executes a Jig" or A.M. Klein's "A Portrait of the Poet as Landscape," have always been marked by a glorious miscegenation of influences; or, to use Peter Van Toorn's words from his 1985 book *Mountain Tea*, "there's always a carnival voice / calling you inside to see the choice / of goods usually hawked at the honeyed / gates of paradise." Heeding this carnival voice has turned the recent scene into a teeming bazaar, where younger poets proudly wear the bright, patchwork clothes of their cosmopolitan nurturing. But something else defines this group. They are the first generation for whom the battle lines of mainstream versus avant-garde (what an earlier time dubbed "cooked" and "raw") have outlived their usefulness. The intense need to set free a shifting sense of self has helped produce the unusual range of devices in this book: intricate puns, up-to-the-minute slang, scat-singing wordplay, many-sided metaphors. These devices are brandished by poets who have not only come out the other side of the poetry wars, but aspire to heal the divisions in their poems. We see this in the cerebral, cubist elegance of Lisa Robertson's "Scene" or the flagrantly self-concious, gear-switching rhymes of Shane Rhodes' "The Paperweight" or the ludic largess of Adam Dickenson's "Call to Arms." These poets belong to a circle that aggressively resist schools, unsettles assumptions and cross-breeds near-infinite varieties of form, from rhyme-rich free verse to mishmashes of lyric and found texts.

Two recent debuts can serve as examples. In *Crabwise to the Hounds* (2008), Jeramy Dodds specializes in densely metaphoric accounts (surrealist tall tales? gothic head trips?) that would look right at home in experimental lit mags like *The Capilano Review* or *Rampike*. But the book also flashes some serious formalist cred, with Ormsbyesque passages that nestle enthusiastically into their internal rhymes, assonances and alliterations ("Capillaries are winter maples scrubbing the mist" or "Shipwrights shoulder-pole / bedrolls and Swede-saws / through a cellophane of rain"). Which is it? Which faction does Dodds belong to? Who knows. It's how poets like him confound that commands our attention. Linda Besner also fails to fit. Her poetry marries a maniacal love for oddity with a loathing for recycled language. One standout in *The Id Kid* (2011) is "Villeneuve Villanelle" in which Besner, who lived in polyglot Montreal for many years, draws on Canada's double heritage of French and English to devise an argot that evades ordinary prose syntax. In the process, she orchestrates an entirely original soundscape:

A van, verily, *une livraison, l'avenir arrived d'ailleurs*, a day

avowed comely, lueur d'avril bespoke, bespilled—*ça brille.*

L'imprévu s'avance impervious; appears apace, *s'est envolé.*

A novice driver, *évidemment*. One *virage rapide*, and all *bouleversé*,
an avalanche of navel oranges *devant la fruiterie*.
A future in delivery, *vraiment*. Moreover, this arrival—*le camion, la journée*—

grand évenement for the vagrants pocketing oranges *à volonté*,
poursuivi by the vainglorious vendor, *à petit avail*. *Ainsi*,
unforeseen advances; *une apparition imperméable* that *vite* blows away.

Une idée, maybe, of ivied-over avenues *à suivre*, asway
with lilas, novelistic verandas. *Rossignols*. Lily-of-the-valley.
En accouchant, l'espoir. Arriving, *d'ailleurs*, a truck, a day *en verité*,

a vaudeville on *la rue* Villeneuve: thrown oranges, oranges *lancées*;
flown oranges, *oranges volées*. Runnelling nuance *d'après ceci*:
une proposition inattendue; ghost in a raincoat, *échappé*.

Abundance, rolling. *Une voie* beloved *d'agrumes*, ravished *d'abeilles*.
And *attendant aux feux*, unbeknownst to driver, fruitman, *sans-abris*:
a van, verily. *Une livraison, l'avenir* arrived *d'ailleurs*—a day
imprévu s'avance impervious. Appears apace; then *envolé*.

One could argue, with justification, that Besner is simply reinventing a traditional
form. But the poem also struck the soi-disant experimental poet Sina Queyras, who
wondered on her blog if "the way this poem is built might be similar to the way
a conceptual poem is built." Queyras' question exposes the grey zone many brash
arrivers—Michael Lista, Joshua Trotter, Leigh Kotsilidis among them—now thrive
in. It's a steampunk zone: populated with lavishly anachronistic, retro-futuristic
inventions—all creolized, vibrant and often intricate. Steampunk was popularized
by speculative works of fiction like William Gibson's *The Difference Engine* (1990)
and Neal Stephenson's *The Diamond Age*. In those books, gadgets of the future are
grafted onto Victorian sensibilities and vice versa. (Imagine Longfellow augmented
by Bluetooth or nanobots in coal clouds.) Our younger poets practice a similar
"path not taken" creativity, defined by salvage and customization, neither backward
or progressive. If Canadian poetry were a sci-fi novel, it would take place in 1900
London with robots, goggle-donning hackers, airships, gear-driven computers and
zombie hordes.

None of this had led to anything you'd call a revolution, though their poems—with their unpredictability, braininess, wisecracks and backtalk—are glimpses of the exhilarating upside-world Canadian poetry might find itself in when completely free of colonial concerns. This current crop of poets don't seem to suffer anxiety about what they do, what's allowable, what tone to take. No one loses any sleep over a reader's confusion. They believe poetry has the power, if not the obligation, to exceed interpretation, and their poems always hunt for larger intellectual frameworks to join (check out the endnotes in their books, which every season grow longer and more esoteric). We once prized homegrown styles cut off from the world. Today the rule is "only connect." No association is too odd or unlikely. Ideas exist in state of high-spirited hyperlinkability.

As a result, more is going on in Canadian poetry than ever before— more sonnets, sestinas, flarf cycles, centos, erasure poems, plunderverse, uncreative writing, concrete. There is also a lot of what no one likes to admit: fatigue. Who can keep up? And for those who try, how does one make sense of it all? Maybe a better way to address this comes from (of all places) the catalogue bumf for Jacob McArther Mooney's 2005 debut *The New Layman's Almanac*. As a poet, Mooney is fascinated by questions of decipherability ("Not the word but the inflec- / tion it presents."), and his poems mull over the results of various kind of reckonings ("1+1-1=1"). The publicity kit picks up on this. "As a collection," we're told, "its primary question is: What are the rules?" This is an excellent question. Much better than claiming there are no rules or insisting we break the rules. This is because "What are the rules?" assumes the existence of a game. (It doesn't hurt that it sounds like something uttered by some poor sod—a friend of a friend, roped in at the last minute—as he's being handed a pile of poker chips.) As it happens, there are basically two kinds of games. Those with rules you need to know before you play them, and those with rules that can only be discovered as you play them. In his indispensible book *Questions of Possibility*, David Caplan argues that "the plurality of alternatives that contemporary poets encounter" has destabilized our sense of "acceptable options." A circumstance, Caplan says, that "makes the poets' formal choices nearly impossible to anticipate." In other words: forget what you know. We've been invited to a game held together by a set of rules that are self-devised, unique, complex and subject to instant change.

Isn't this, in a sense, what I've always wanted? Yes. It's been our destiny ever since the mongrel brilliance of E.J. Pratt's gigantic, fast-paced verse-narratives began appearing one hundred years ago. So why am I glum? Because while our poetry is now home to ravishingly odd confections, and while many of these poems bring me under their spell, they never quite make the sale. I'm pushover for anything "counter, original, spare, strange," as Hopkins put it. I read such poems for matters of style, of sound. I read to understand why I like what I do, why some poems seem to me more memorable than others. I read, ultimately, to take this knowledge into my own poems. But after a point, after celebrating the explosion of poetic techniques, I have to ask myself: what are all those techniques *for*, exactly? Jonathan Ball's Borgesian *Clockfire* (2010) was an exceptionally interesting book: 77 impossible-to-stage plays ("The audience enters the theatre. One at a time. As they enter, they are slaughtered.

The curtain hangs in mid-air.") Yet a part of me fears this is poetry in the same way short-selling is considered legal: by the skin of its teeth. W. H. Auden once described his dream reader as someone who cherished "curious prosodic fauna like bacchics and choriambs." But bacchics and choriambs are worthless unless they're intrinsic to the perception that seeks them out; unless they're essential for minting a specific kind of meaning—a sharpness of feeling, an urgency—that those devices, and only those devices, make possible. *Clockfire* is Ball's version of Auden's bacchics and choriambs. The book is its own nonce form, and as such, a steampunk act of conceptual savvy; a cool idea, well-executed. But is it the by-product of a poet getting into deep trouble? The function of a mind grappling at genuinely felt expression? Am I the only one who found himself impressed, then distressed that I could grasp a great deal about the poems, except why they were written?

I don't mean to pick on Ball, who is one of our most talented younger poets, but to use his fascinating book to make a larger point: that there's difference between a game and a poem. Both should be played with as much skill as possible, but a game is played for it's own sake, while a poem, and our pleasure in its gambits, depends on the recognition it is saying something true about life. A poem, essentially, is a game with a single price of admission: that its rules aren't cut off from the sadness, exultation or distress that pushed the poet to fashion those rules in the first place. I've reconciled myself to the fact that we've moved past poetry as the zero-sum sport Frost called "prowess—something to achieve, something to win or lose." Yet we seem pretty far from the only other option likely to generate memorable work: the clue-gathering Auden called the "game of knowledge, a bringing to consciousness, by naming them, of emotions and their hidden relationships."

A poem, according to Auden's formulation, comes to a head. It's a breakthrough into clarity that draws together the maximum information available. This requires us to believe words aren't just what they do, but what they mean; that form isn't just an R&D staging area—will popping in this stanzaic shape make the poem more acoustically untypical?—but embodies a sense of responsibility for the effects being created in other minds. Gregory Betts' *The Others Raised in Me* (2010) is collection of 150 poems that cuts and remixes words found in Shakespeare's Sonnet 150. Matthew Tierney's *The Ides* uses software to record 20 seconds of audio from the radio, which he then transcribes onto an Excel spreadsheet and tags according to various criteria. In each case, the results have been fascinating. But what untrendy mystery, what human plight, hope or grief have these projects brought to consciousness? Yes, I get it: the goal, in part, is to escape the trap of the already-done. But even so, what are the stakes? Why should we care? Is all that steampunking being applied to profound ends or merely skin-deep? To be sure, what appears to drive Betts and Tierney is anything but trivial: to rebuild the foundations of the lyric from scratch, to submit their nonpareil concoctions as counterprogramming for the Canadian canon. And yet that strikes me as the easy part; made obvious by the scores of poets doing it. Such poetry is frequently over-deliberate; a didactic version of originality, one that keeps insisting on its novelty. Much of it testifies, at best, to the presence of a creative habit, but not the intensity of art. Diction and syntax are paired up in distractingly pleasant, half-lucid marriages which rarely achieve the organization and intention required for poetry. Umberto Eco has called this drug "suggestive verbalism" and too many Canadian poets are hooked on it. The real game of writing poetry remains the part that rests entirely on a lucky break: the creation of a singular, standalone word structure that satisfies emotionally and intellectually while signaling itself as an artifice.

Have our poets been that lucky? Absolutely. I love the backbone Asa Boxer puts into his hunches: he produces uncannily precise images that grow out his intuitions about sound. If you find yourself unexpectedly moved by Amanda Jernigan lines it's largely due to the way she has streamlined her statements but doubled their aural weight: everything is sadder because the words are crisper. I marvel over how Nyla Matuk can dress abstractions in sensualized details and how her surrealistic thinking moves crabwise; cross-referring, branching out. What ultimately lingers aren't her insights—which land cleanly and memorably—but the thought-process whose zigs and zags are their own reward. Or Karen Solie, whose brainy verse-patterns decode emotions to a chill clarity. The result: black humour, a discreetly rich pessimism, and a mind in constant, fascinated dialogue with its own disappointments. Bruce Taylor has patented a new genre: the meditative cliffhanger. His poems take the shape of an idea or mood clarifying itself in stages, leaving readers on tenterhooks to find out where he'll go next. Hairpin enjambment—every line taking a sharp left turn—is the most recognizable suspense-building feature, giving the poems a jaggedly uneven look. Visually, this advertises his quick reflexes, but also a living sense of form: Taylor adds new lines to pull new ideas in, allowing him to continuously refresh what he is thinking. As a result, his poems never feel like they are created top-down, from a concept, but bottom-up, one word at a time.

But, just as often, Canadian poets don't play the odds as much as stack the deck. As more of them keep one eye on the lyric tradition and one eye on whatever comes next, they increasingly try to force a breakthrough by splitting the difference. The result can be too perfect, as if it were the winner of a contest to compose the ideal hybrid poem. Dickinson has a project called *Anatomic: Semiotic Bodies, Chemical Environments* for which he plans to subject himself to exhaustive chemical testing. Why does he intend to do this? "By making a map of the toxicological and symbiotic circumstances of my body," he says, "I want to then use this information to create methodologies for producing poems." Whether Dickinson's "methodologies" will produce good poems remains to be seen, but so unimpeachably does his super-experiment ape the terms of what we now expect from our poems, the venture lives in its own hybridized universe. Indeed, the dominance of the steampunk aesthetic, the easy availability of its procedures, has led to a growing uncertainty about how to discuss such linguistic lab-work, or even whether anything meaningful can be said at all. The entrepreneurial spree of poets patenting new forms, and the feeling of optimism and copiousness that accompanies it, overwhelms taste. When every poet happens to be writing exactly the kind of poem he or she set out to write, and every poem embodies exactly its theoretical intent, it becomes harder to say which poems are good, and why; how one kind of recombining and estranging differs from another; what books are truly counter, original, spare, strange.

In practical terms, the situation has left reviewers, editors and anthologists scrambling to describe poems in ways they hope will pique the curiosity of readers. That means, too often, sentences are variations on "so-and-so's poetry exists in the middle ground between tradition and innovation." Period styles in poetry in other words, beget period styles in poetics. In our case, criticism becomes a kind of catechism, a reiteration of steampunk principles. Take Jeff Latosik who describes Dodds as "One half the muscular lyricism of a Ken Babstock or Karen Solie and one half the unfettered linguistic play of a Christian Bök or Margaret Christakos." Or Rhodes' publisher NeWest who says he "combines moving lyrical poetry with experimental verve." Indeed, when even an excellent critic like Zachariah Wells is compelled to characterize Trotter's poetry as "mix[ing] the anti-matter of postmodern language games and shifty subjectivity with the matter of traditional structures and lyric poignancy" you realize no one is immune. Such explication, however well meant, is so far removed from what the poetry is actually doing that it becomes a way of concealing a vacancy in our thinking. The area between tradition and innovation is an intellectual fiction: you cannot go there to write poems. It doesn't exist. What *does* exist is the thousands of ways poets compose with and against the formulas available in English. You cannot, a priori, negotiate a trade-off between round avant peg and square trad hole. One *can* invent a voice that catches the friction between carefully crafted structure and spontaneous departure. Indeed the pervasiveness of terms like "hybrid," "plurality" and elliptical"—or what Ron Silliman calls "third-wave poetics" and Jay Millar calls "retro avant garde" and Queyras calls the "avant lyric"—marks a new conventional wisdom that is part conviction, part guff, part make-believe. And as intellectual thresholds are reduced to practically zero, we are fast approaching a kind of free economy: it costs nothing to blog about these things. God knows it means nothing.

There's a lovely image in William Gibson's novel *Count Zero* (1986) of a sentient computer deep in an abandoned space station, creating beautiful Cornell boxes out of junk. The boxes make it into the hands of admiring art dealers on Earth who are unaware of their provenance. In the same way, Canadian poets generate, as if on automatic, wonderful contrivances from disparate materials. These are poets who care about their poetry and work hard at it. Like watchmakers, they build machines out of the minutest parts; unlike watches, these machines are full of beguiling generosity for errant incidents. But too often we are faced with an artificial intelligence, simulated for believability, not an actual style. Style is what happens when originality becomes indistinguishable from the poem itself. It's a way of mingling the unfamiliar "new" and the still-compelling "old" so that we can no longer separate them. Style is therefore what happens when a voice is so grounded in its subject the effect is not a self-regarding newness but a newness absorbed into the poem, a newness ripening into something effortlessly manifold and available. Such poems may not be the sort fusionists like, but they are the sort real poets write.

The Best Canadian Poetry in English 2012

Salvador Dali Lama

I am the Salvador Dali Lama, shake my hand
marvel at my power, shake my hand
let lobsters now be telephones, wave my hand

invite twelve more for dinner, I will be the thirteenth
the betrayer, for that is my great genius
mixing religions with metaphors, mixing oils
slick back my hair, stroke my moustache, where's your wife
she will die and be reborn as mine, my Gala Lama

you didn't look her in the eyes, I see nothing else
I barely see her breasts, look at her eyes
I will put her in a painting, edges blurred
but those eyes sharp, tigers leaping from fish

I am the Salvador Dali Lama, shake my hand
all dogs are Andalusian, wave my hand
let all ages be golden, wave my hand
in robes of shadows, melted watches on my chest
pulling me down, from melted trees, dripping earth

in eggshell worlds, on the backs of elephants
legs all the way to Heaven, virgins break
I will be reborn as nothing, will made perfect
ants crawling out of my head, freed from want

I am the Salvador Dali Lama, shake my hand
the world is made of nightmares, take my hand
all of the faces are mine, or my mother's
all of them laughing, all at different things

Wartime Puppet Play Of The Kitchen Stove

To fight with bowl and arrow, mustard seed and gas. To the
Northeast the crockery clashed, tea-towels bannering while
Renegade kernels whistled dixie south of the Mason jar line.
Fallen to the foxhole basin drain the pierced sieve gurgling
Hundredfold to black. The peppermill lighthoused a warning:
GADZOOKS! Through five-alarm smoke, four raging bull's-eyes
Brayed from pea-green fields aflame to Oxo cubes penned in and
Bleating. Behind the wall, the voices of disembodied mice
Uplifted with the tin can resistance in their banned anthem,
La Mayonnaise.
In the fallout a scuttled Bialetti slept on the sandscuffed rim.
The demobbed double boiler, its cold helmet fogged yet with
Flashbacks of dead steam, huddled thinking: For them; for their
Thankless foppish freedom those nigger wop commie jews...
No warmth from the citadel where sickly butter hid.
In the pockmarked plain of the ashen range, the dusty dishrag
Wrung its black-and-white checks. Knelt alone repeating to the fan
Blowing the all clear, La afham. La a'ref. La adri.
(I don't understand. I don't know. I have no idea.)

Gardening

Under the foxgloves, worms. A white
gleam writhes, cut, under the shovel.

What I doubled multiplies down there
below what I thought I made good.

The Beach is a Rake

Extending a limb, the tide
tests and tests again the texture

of the sand, then mounts, dissolves
upheavals and castles of grit.

Where water passes, beach brims
and sparkles, relaxing back

into himself. For the next
million years, she will bank

on him; he will break her.
He clumps when she is gone.

He grows shifty and dun.
He hides money, dirty habits.

She sifts his cockles, uncovers
oysters and mother-of-pearl.

The Breakup of the Ice on the Tidnish River

(for Amber)

"When she goes, she all goes out at once,"
my uncle said the Friday I arrived;
and Sunday half the family watched it go:
like freight cars rolling from the train's last shunt,
slow-moving tons of slushy ice floes.
Bound by the cold habit of foot-thick ice
all winter long, the water swelled and sighed
in secret for the moon. The only sign

the little river's breathing had kept time
with tidal rhythms were her ragged banks
where edges of the unrolled, broad, blank
bolt of heavy winter cloth had frayed
at the friction of the river's rise and fall.
"But now, with ice around the *Wabash* broke,
the dregs of winter's gonna wash away."

It was my father's sixtieth that week,
and all his kids and grandkids had come down
to his half-brother's place as a surprise:
my brother from Toronto with both children;
my sister from the Valley with her three;
and me, still on my own, from Montreal.
Dad and Les drove up from Saint John.
In just one generation we had spread
cross half the country, stretching family ties
so far and thin so long, some naturally snapped
or wore away; some, like Via tracks,
were just torn up, the station left to rot
or sold to Tim Horton's as a coffee shop.
There'd been successes, healthy kids and luck,
but losses too, and changes souls felt they were owed:
the unforgiving fault line of divorce;
the old black hole of poverty and debt;
not seeing the way that person turned that day;
learning we've not loved enough, and won't;
so what was left of family ties might seem
a hand-patched fishnet beached in flotsam.

As close as we could get to what could pass
for home was now with relatives along
the Isthmus of Chignecto where the Tidnish ran.
It's here we'd come by train or car or plane

to give our father his best April Fool's.
I came in first, alone, to ease the shock
of the joke we'd pulled on Dad, who hardly had
the chance to catch his breath when the door gave in,
a flooded dyke, to all five grandchildren.
Dad had never been with all the kids
at once; nor had my sister ever gone
to him since she'd left home, and he our Mom.

The party was the Friday night in town.
On Saturday we toured the sugar bush:
Hansels and Gretels all, we trailed blue tap-
lines through the well-groomed woods to the sugar shack
beside the pond that spins the water-wheel
and watched the wood fire boil down the sap
to maple butter, fudge and golden syrup.

By Sunday afternoon we had to leave.
We lunched last at my uncle's out of town
beside the river, which was also on
the run and packing up her winter bags.
Everything flows.
                    As parents milled and mulled
about the kitchen, tending to themselves,
the kids ran headlong to the riverbank,
all set for adventure at the edge
of dark, ice-laden water on the ebb.
I went along to give the parents some
time off and me the time to play at Dad.

The kids are running up and down the riverbank;
they're chucking sticks into the water, kicking ice
floes from the edge and jumping on the undone dock.
And I imagine them imagining a quest
into our wasted North, the damsel in distress,
the hero dancing 'cross an iceberg just in time.
Their game is just as dangerous. Then I'm
all eyes and caution and anxiety.

The floes, the kids, the tide, the river run;
shrinking sheets of ice, snow banks in ruins
are glaring back at me as sunlight scatters flash
across the river, off a thousand waves

as small as children's hands—that silver rush
the wind shakes from a stand of poplar trees.
At arm's length, all I have and haven't known
of kids and family is just beyond
my reach and slipping further from me. I come
up empty-handed every time I flail
around to ward the children, as in those failed
embraces in the Underworld.

That weekend Dad kept saying he kept on seeing
his grandkids come to greet him in his dreams.
I will see the backs of children's heads
going out of focus in the dazzling light.

Salvage

You can tell a thousand-footer
by her straight back, hammer head
—a skyscraper toppled.
Too long for locks, what she's best at:
pushing taconite from Duluth to Gary,
the endless circuitry of ports.
Built from the centre of the earth up,
this ship is a piece of ceremonial armour,
a leviathan penny, a horseshoe
pinned to Great Lakes lucky until she's not.
Christened and kissed off
years before you were born,
she is an older sister, a summer cousin
who only appears in a quarter of your photos
and out of focus. She's your favourite
because you barely know her.
In smaller water, this ship could be
an island, bridge, or territory.
She is a herd of 20,000 horses
trembling to shake off its load.
In her wake, lesser vessels are sent to scrap,
run aground, and peeled down to air, yet one day
it will cost less to wreck her than to keep her:
a final trip to Port Colborne or Alang.
Breakers will scrabble up her hard-rusted sides,
pull her down by torch and hand.
Her pieces soon held in the gut
of another ship downbound for better things.

After Edwin H. Gott

Call To Arms

The highway rollover wore him
like a loose jacket, a wind-snapped flag,
like a rodeo bull wears a cowboy,
sanded him down until his arms
were dusted off, re-written
in fibreglass and hooked script.
We were frightened by his make-believe hands,
smooth upholstery knuckles, unflinching
beach ball smell backed
by baked bicycle tires.
We were frightened of the fishing trip
and the lightning that welded
him to the boat.
We were frightened of those shoulders
retrofitted into clothes hangers
for broken handshakes and bear hugs,
dialled phones and signatures
packed away into boxes
for accountants or the poor.
We practiced our own substitutions,
acting out ghost stories, declaring allegiance
to phantom limbs
while playing high-kick soccer,
awarding exaggerated penalties
for handballs,
offenders chicken-winged
and forced to pirate copies
of hoof-and-mouth disease
for overseas quarantined manicurists.
We wore hand-me-down turtlenecks
and packed scavenged finger-food
for the sergeant-at-Arms.
In the sawtoothed canines,
masticating above us in climax beech leaf canopies,
we saw vestigial forests
of terminal arm hair, small sod
melanin huts, knob and kettle country
in the vascular ridgelines.
We took flu shots to change our appearance
on the inside, planted memories
of synthetic identities, dusted for fingerprints
in unauthorized hands.
Climbing through polite conversation,

we wore nosebleeds to conceal our altitude,
fake moustaches to hide harelips we`d affected
for counterfeit phonemes, and slipped
into pairs of scissors,
hiding in roughhouses built by play-facing dogs
and the first-draft carbon crystals
of burnt-out engine blocks.
We raised branches from sticks
and trained them into tepees and log houses
for bonfires,
schooled them
in the relative humilities for dry rot.
We placed orange peels
over our eyes and groped
for light sockets,
donned dandelion manes
and crawled through switchblade grasses
with sextants certifying the sky
for seeds.
Having had our wrists slapped,
we grew polycarbonate cups
out of sight in the carpal tunnels
and drank under water tables
at night, where we`d beat snowstorms
to death with flashlights
and proclaim republics
on the accumulated evidence of road salt
and body-counted shadow puppets.
We wore intestinal flora
on our sleeves
as a countermeasure against
the invisible hand of decompositional self-interest.
We hung out with stray dogs
who did all of our terrifying
for us.
The one with three legs limped along
like a pitchfork, its tines tuned
to the hiss of escaped air
from pierced plastic balls.
Back and forth its head swung
ripping apart a cloud
or a man's shirt.

The Swan with Two Necks

The loveliest bird of Franguestan!
—Lord Byron

You may've heard before now, two better than one moms say
But as Christopher Walken and I were walking one day
We got to talking of the pond-giraffes lobbying off-shore
So serene up top, even though below their legs scuttled and tore
The pond's surface – like pack ice with periscopes loosed
From a glacier's lip – until a bleach-blonde with her dog noosed
In its leash screamed and barked as some four-breasted beast
Burst from the deep and with Gorgon squawks creased
Our pleasant Sunday, like the linen suit I slept in for weeks.

That Layer of Leda, a Child of Chernobyl, an eyesore.
Throats flailing like unmanned firehoses at full-bore, or
Two tenors in tantrum; beaks braying like Kraken-sired foals
In a canyon of crystal bells where kamikazes collect the tolls.
The mauve purse of each bill begging for bankruptcy
As Walken and I ran to flee this garden-gone-Gethsemane;
Flaneurs folded at the knees when Olde Two-Beaks reached as one
And, with fine Siamese formation, deboned that blonde's Dalmatian,
Dolling its dim innards out as alms for a cavernous sun—

Just as the Oracle at Delphi would've done at each demi-god's
Birth – then, swirling its cotton candy girth, whipsawed
The pond's skin of paddle boaters and bathers like a surgeon
Swipes a dining table for the impromptu caesarean
Of a stillborn unicorn, or twin-breeched cherubim.
That saw-toothed soothsayer tweezed the gamey limbs
Off a dozen or so park-loving souls, shot-gunning gushes
Of arterial spray and re-planting each limbs as bulrushes
Or five-fingered crocuses, bejeweling the rim of such and such's

Octopied garden. Seeing this, Chris cussed a Thesian vow
Of violence: to gut-weave it an entrails wedding train. Now,
Tossing me the keys, Chris cartwheeled into our El Camino's
Bed. As the camera phones panned in arms-length slow-mo
I godsped off the dock, transforming our truck into
A half-bred fossil-fueled warhead, catapulting Chris onto
Those wily albino adders now madder than method actors
Typecast as whores even the Marquis de Sade couldn't adore.
Chris, pancaking out of his somersault and into a soar,

Drew his Douk-Douk mid-flight, its blade bright as matchstrike.
Second only to the sun as he socked it to the fridge-white
Right throat of that shift-shaped chimera. Twisting his wrist
Till the knife turned to a zipper's tongue in his cinched fist,
Chris carved down, halving half our fiend from gullet to gizzard
Just as our truck struck like a crane-dropped crate in the freightyard
And smithereened. Petroleum flames phoenixed our fiend in a jiff,
Though its alive side s-bent and bullwhipped, gator-clipping my midriff
As I tried to front-crawl away, flicking me inshore as if

I were a ball-jointed doll not-to-scale with its too-tall
Twin-towering maws. As if I'd brought the right one's fall.
Leaving the left alone to wail, Chris swam up its rear
Ramp of tail feathers, shimmying the enflamed throat–near
Retardant in his asbestos overcoat–his Douk-Douk
A pike-diving diamond cleaving that fiend's soot toque
Flaying its tonsils, gelding its brasswind cannonade-croak
Into a scat-talked castrato. Fire-polling that enflamed throat
Chris landed on a bulkhead hatch beneath its singed coat—

A coat like the wing cloak Daedalus designed for his Fall line.
Can-opening the hatch, a black, smoke-blouse bellied, as turbines
Unwound, axletrees cracked. And Chris soon saw, low and behold,
once the smoke left home, Cate Blanchett and Tilda Swinton pinfolded
To a dial-caked panel that sparked and arc-welded their bilging eyes,
Water geysering up gearboxes, antifreeze greasing their thighs.
Then the sump-pumps of both Báthorian queens hydralicked
A last time as the Dopplers chimed, kerplunking in a palsied fit
That beast sunk to the pond's underscore. All this due to a verdict

Laid down by our Oracle Oprah: "The champagne of all
Anti-aging creams comes from the distilled blood of liberal
Democrats relaxed by a pond's dulcet lap." Only when
Chris finally felt his loss, I was found, deep in the fen
Lying so casual-like but for my cummerbund of blood,
My large intestine toilet-papering a nearby shrub.
Under the woodchuck woodchuck of helicopters in the sky
He held me, fist pumping, asking the gods, Why
When Charon bid me aboard had I so blindly said aye, aye?

I'd lived best supporting, but in death nailed the lead. It had
Been an especially dangerous scene, but I had had
The guts to lock my stand-in stunt man in a port-a-potty

And, with a little make up, stood in for myself. A flea
Cast as itself by default acts out its wildest dreams.
Now, a jillion earthworms perch at my casket's seams
While Chris chisels this on my headstone shellacked in sun-sheen
And a writhing half-moon of bikini-clad teens scream:
One day, my friends, we all must step out of our machines.

True Confession

Really we should try to love each other less,
opt for regular spells of independence.
I'm perfectly fine without you, I confess.

Tired of all these games of chance and guess?
Relationships are always meant to fence us.
Really we should try to love each other less.

Love's too full of all that thrust and press—
strange controlling my-way-only dance.
I'm free and fine without you, I confess.

I'm off to wander in the wilderness,
some quiet hamlet in the south of France.
I really need some space to love you less.

No use this lovey-dovey, kiss, caress.
I'd rather poke my eyes out with a lance.
I'm better off without you, I profess.

Okay, admit it, our lives are in a mess,
as bad as Guildenstern or Rosencrantz.
I need you just a little, I confess.
Really I should try to lie a little less.

Dish Bitches

Every boomerang I toss
wobbles off to clobber a neighbour.

My stack of stapled job apps
circles back to chain me to this sink of steel—

Elbow-deep in foaming pots
scraping veal and apricots

From dented pans and countertops…
Half-asleep at work, I'm dreaming

Jungle rivers, sleeping with a tiger,
not holding down a job

That goes nowhere,
chops the air,

And wanders back into your hands,
willy-nilly.

It can never be satisfied, the mind,
not really.

Solstice Night

A blue lake surrounds the house: snow
restored by twilight to a version of its original self,
stippled where wind and animals have crossed,
barred by shadows of trees.
And speaking of trees, shadows fly out from them
like time-traces of late-summer bats, and return.
Everything dampens down.
A sudden stillness—
and the earth's tilt reverses.
Gradually the first stars prick the sky around the moon's pearled curve.
The last of the year's scrap wood is ready for burning.

Also a twilight everything turns from:
stamping our feet on the platform waiting for the train,
lined up on the curb waiting for the bus, blowing on our fingers.
Young men shaking snow from their collars
as they pass through turnstiles and descend
with everyone else into the tunnels and shopping concourses,
into the wet stink, the grit and slush, blasts of heat and noise
over the hornet-hum of earbuds and ringtones, ignoring
everything, which is a form of love—

Arm in arm a young couple stand in front of a window
brimming with tiny confections. He pulls off her hat—
a sudden stillness—
then breathes into the gold waves of her hair.
And night opens before them like a dinner napkin,
like a carousel starting up, night as a state,
moonless, starless, yet spangling. We're burning
everything we have. We're cheering ourselves on.

Say Here, Here

Say cloverleaf, polyethylene. Say this parking lot
slinks into marshland, bristles into scrubland.
Say this mall becomes the world's biggest bonfire
and you travel its plastic smoke.

Say sky, fescue, say Wîsahkêcâhk,
say La Vérendrye and Henday,
say heart-choke, say groundbreak, say garrison
with gunbarrel eyes, say there's a fist
yelling this is my apartment now in a language
you don't know, say geno- matri- patri-
cide, say regicide, say terracide and skyocide,
say sapling, say childblood, cry doctor,
say your piece then get out, say translate, please
translate. Say coyote, say smallpox, say
creekbottom, look, Wîsahkêcâhk.

Say Big Bear.

Say Frog Lake, say fresh loam, say buffalo
hide, say free land, say thistle, aspen, sweat.
Riel, say Riel
can govern in Michif,

say colour, say colour-
less eye, say Queen's portrait, say here, here
is mine I bought it, say settler, claim
poverty, say better and see the felled trees,
say brethren, bread and wagons,
say Spanish flu, say railyard, sing
the combustion engine, say the singing
of your name in the new air, say virgin
territory and believe it, say the Lord's
bounty, say the wheatfields, say the dust,
pick the rocks, say canola and soybean,
thresh, thrush, say the laundry
on the line, say the dank root cellar,
say the numbers, tell the wheat board
where to go, say it fast like an auction and move

to the city, say minimum wage and grunt while you work,
say benefits, say rigpig derrick oilsand tailings pond boom,
say busted skull, say tuition fund and heritage fund, say concrete

scaffold, say it far from home, say the length of your commute
at the sound of the tone, say Ralph Klein and spit in the dirt.

Say Skydancer, say Zwicky, say
Alberta and Saskatchewan then
switch the order.

Say Wayne Gretzky Drive, say it's five-on-three
and he's on a break-away, scream it
in the riot on Canada Day, whisper it into your pilsner,
say it from the hollow of the couch, say it while you piss in the alley,
hiss it into your lover's ear,
say it to your broker and his secretaries, tell it to the lawyer,
to the landlord when the heat's shut off and the pipes freeze,
say it again to the food bank and again to the caseworker,

say cloverleaf highway polyethylene grocery sack.
Say fluorescent lightbulbs will save the earth, say there's a heart
in the middle of it (please tell me you can hear it),
say glut and democracy, say it in absentia,
say your little heartbeat, say it through the layers,
say it in the smoke of this blank, this bristling parking lot.

Corrections

My friend works medium security and says
of his mad charges, "You can't be angry.
They're sick—shouldn't be here." To the near-sane,
he doles punishments when " Fuck you, screw"
is prelude to a shank – some soup spoon snatched
and ground against the whetstone of the bars,
a razor blade bound into a pencil's
eraser tip, or merely the handle
of a toothbrush made sharp as murder-one.
And stranger things: back in stir after
his biopsy a man threatened to force
a pen through the hole and crush his liver
unless given Tylenol Three. He settled for
Extra Strength and the promise of a doctor:
"I was just joking," he added meekly,
knowing threats of self-harm bring sanctions too—
days apart in an observation cell,
diaper-clad and deprived of any thing
imagination could turn into a noose.
Others would cut themselves or even rip
open the skin and muscle with their hands;
one inmate slashed deeper than his scrotum,
poured blood and half his entrails on the floor;
luckless, he missed the artery and lived.
Some lifers, almost done, can no longer mount
the stairs to the range or have left their
wits at the scene – time's muddled fugitives
who could not pick themselves from a line–up.
Beyond correction, a man with one leg
weighs 500 pounds and may no longer lift
himself. Torpid, he pisses and shits among
the blankets, cannot wash or move,
cuffed to a history of offences,
manslaughter (released) and then child rape.
His heart and kidneys wind down – my friend,
tall as a linebacker, joins a staggering
scrimmage of guards and paramedics,
as they hoist the stretcher down stairwells
and across a lighted courtyard to the gate
where an ambulance waits to parole him.

The Tank

Squats three days at a time in white-brown mud
that sticks and sucks, like a mouth, against
everything it touches. The long battle,
the bit-by-bit of urging steel to the centre
of the earth. You dream of sinking, past
the slow riot of oil, sand and stone,
to the bottom of the prairie shield.

Rig out. The pylons packed, extinguishers
strapped, the guy wires of the stack, plucked,
swing loose again against the sky. Everything ends,
briefly, and the iron world moves on.

Only the tire ruts are left, six inches
deep, wet with water and an oil sheen,
and even these are eaten over by wheat
and flax and mustard seeds.

No mark survives this place: you too will yield
to unmemory. Give everything you are
in three-day pieces. Watch the gypsy-iron
move, follow its commands.
Tend the rusted steel like a shepherd.

X-Ray

So this is where I've hidden
my ghost, shadow of all

my firsts, essential self
shuttered down to its most

basic pajamas:
I've been looking for you,

ornithological bouquet
blooming in the dark

room of my days,
I've been walking around

in negative,
I've been wondering

how I fit, moony
white, in the wetsuit of my body –

so it's good
to greet you at last,

and to see
there's nothing wrong

with me, nothing
broken, nothing missing

but the wings
of a book

in my hand, nothing
but a little

lamplight
left on inside me.

Aubade

The time, if time it was, would ripen
in its own sweet time. One thought of dawn.
One felt that things were shaping up,
somehow, that it was getting on.

Day broke. Upon the waters broke
in waves on waves unbreaking and
night fell, unveiling in its wake
one perfect whitened rib of land.

I slept, and while I slept I dreamed,
a breaking wave, a flowering tree,
and all of one accord I seemed.
I woke, and you divided me.

Inland

Pull me out of the aircrash
Pull me out of the lake
       —Radiohead

1.

Left unaided to temper the seam of
a mechanical wing, we release our
cloak-pins, set to kindling flares. Above
jays alight where earlier we scoured
the heavens for cover, the heavens gone
dark over solitary tracks. Exiled,
grounded in bile, piss; our maps redrawn
on survey; we limp from the audible
hiss of the river, fuselage flooding
with surf. Here remnants console, stir
our hunger for beauty: razed shells, studs,
rosin spilled on contact with an arbor
of pine. Negotiating distance, flames
diverge, forsake the sky for coming rain.

2.

Flames diverge, forsake the sky; a bitter
plinth of sun. It seems an age we spurned
the earth, its bow and quake, tow interred
in the ocean's relief. '41; terns
rose from Bonavista Bay, clipped Banting
in escort to the Old World. Light work
his drop, his desperation. Winter's slant
right angled into passage; the same fork
that drew our *Beaver* to mire, united
wheel and weight. Newly
transient we cling to suitcases like
folding armor; Ulysses' kin rowing
our breastplates to shore. Instrument, hostile
lover, we follow the river for miles.

3.
Love, we follow the river for miles:
cut nascent tracks, pace its glacial shell.
A day, two perhaps, and fever riles
our guts, sets my compass to a hell
renewed by famine. Fireweed, black spruce,
balsam: frozen talismans, paperweights
we plunder for a means to heal. No use
tunneling, worrying winter's seal; hate
gives way to panic, metal to bark; form
deformed with each inexpert blow.
I gasp, newly pneumonic, a storm
of alveolar blood spewed-up in snow:
clots softened, excess a lithograph we
inhabit with a leper's mastery.

4.

Smoke a lithograph, a leper's signal
we've learned to distrust. Miles back, rain
spoiled our carrion; its diurnal
warning dispersed like a peacock drained
of color. And what of winter's soot,
our haven's upturned roots? Before us,
the Appalachians lift above the foot-
hills, mute our shovels; our ex-pilot
bared of his rifle and interred in a
makeshift shroud. Ornament, his gun, without
ammunition; trigger an apical
tick, comfort surrendered to frostbite, gout.
When coyotes near our camp we depart,
their cries revelatory, claws alert.

5.

Our cries are revelatory, hopeful
at the first hint of an enclosure.
Closer, an orphaned cow emerges; dull
eyes fenced in a sash of fur, burrs
obscuring recognition. A sure thing,
domesticity, the span of rail
assembled to betray our wandering.
Network of decay, ancestry, veil.
Sea-light despite the ocean's darkening
cloak, our estuary's muddy tongue.
Overhead, revelation's ruddy mark
extends like venom, an unnoticed hue:
flame kindled to ablate
an abandoned foundation, *tout suite.*

6.

An abandoned foundation: barrow,
manure, fiberglass; furnace oil
echoing my hand at flint: now, now,
now and the otherness of fire, soil
soldered to the cabin's melted ground-
work. Unbridled, we set our mark upon
this domicile like mutts; dogs wounding
dogs until Penelope's arrow yawns
and collapses in a rut. God's tinder-
box an unsteady muse, a lapse in prayer:
for thine is the kingdom, the disorder
in my breast for ever and ever.
Anchored to our disgrace, we bend
to tame the river's flux. Somnambulant.

7.

Grace. A helicopter tames the river's
flux, lumbers over a flock of trailing
geese. At last we forgo deliverance,
nature's trespass; the crux of our failure
a few sticks of wood, the plateau of green
where we regenerate, birdlike.
Everywhere at once, the weather's mean:
flatlands furrowed, windows spiked
with hail; marram resistant as we bi-
sect the horizon. Monastic blades
fashion a cross over the sun. Scythe
hearted, our company's shade
lifts likeness from stands of birch, blots
retreating lanes of wind: our pilot.

8.

Effaced by retreat, lanes of wind fix
our flag to Pearson's tarmac: one and one
and one seeding backfields with brick
and bone. In abeyance, bridges have gone
slack; my return clubfooted, barbed
with disease. *Fee-fi-fo-fum*, I crop my
beard like an Englishman. Scissored, I cede
to instinct: finally barefoot, propped
against a bathroom mirror. Charged to strip
the dirt from my reflection I leave
the worry to my double, drift
towards a single mattress, the quiet cave
of your arms. Pieced together like worms,
we resist exchange. The sun tempers our seams.

By Any Name

When jackals' baying is both backdrop
and foreground, when forest

is conifers and impenetrable
fence, when mongoose predator

equals mongoose prey, which truth
will the brain feign?

A lyrebird's call appropriates
any sound it fancies. Above us,

shithawks flock
to mock us. Featherbrained,

we agree bullshit is the best
decoy. The average vocabulary

is 10,000 words, and one
easily stands in for another.

It is all the same.
For example, you, me

and the Cecropia moth,
born speechless, wriggling

free, only to flop atop
the first moth we see.

from Care Package for a Combat Engineer

1. Items the Curiosity Cabinet at the Redpath Museum

Fragment of a triceratops skull, not to be
mistaken for shrapnel.

Emerald feather plucked
from the worse-for-wear tail
of a Carolina parakeet, extinct
since the Great War. (It might
have adorned a hat.)

A calcite specimen chunked
with dolomite, donated by D. Doell,
who spotted it some decades back
at Sainte-Clotilde-de-Chateauguay,
where it loomed aside the path,
a misshapen mishmash threatening
to mutate. Before walking on,
he cradled it and dropped it
in his sack.

(See how it didn't blow up? He didn't
even suspect it.)

Take care with this spike I plucked
from the spiny echidna: an egg-laying,
Tasmanian mammal equipped with a snout,
beak and 18-inch tongue that whips
hideouts clean (anthills, I mean).

No one saw me chip a corner off
some glistening Chinese stibnite:
angular and metallic, tinged
black. The thing scared me. Think
petrified kindling. Charred
highrises in a heap. Rifle necks
poking through rubble.

And check this out: an ocarina
with bent knees, flat ears, a Garfield girth,
broken nose and missing left foot.
Blow a tune through the hole
in its head, tap along the eye slits,

three circular chest wounds,
the hollow in its butt—

which may give rise to a few
one-liners, maybe clear the air
in the stuffy mud compound
where you're stationed. Call these playthings
or paperweights. Whistles,
lucky charms. You

with your pocketknife and practical ways,
my better-than-MacGyver, my emergency-candle
lantern-supplier, my avalanche-risk-
analyzer-with-weatherproof-pen, who tucks
condoms under the pillow and keeps
an earthquake supply of condensed milk,
who checks the forecast and respects
the rhythms of cats, you'll know

what to do. I send you these remnants,
all this evidence.

2. Anti-scurvy Rations Supplement Kit from the Montreal Botanical Gardens

Their backs were turned, so I raided
the garden of edible flowers. I was armed.
In my satchel, Type II, Style A, Flavour 1
kippered beef snack. *C'est pour un soldat.*
He's on vacuum-sealed entrées—vous
voyez? Their chins dropped. They uprooted
beds of violas and zinnias, then, like harried
babcias, tied them in plastic bags,
strapped them to my waist, kissed
me twenty times and sent me

home. Here you are. Each rosehip
packs a dose of vitamin C. Marigolds too,
but ugh, bitter. Per linden, one mouthful
of honey. Sweet woodruff's a nutty dessert.
Chicory, every soldier knows, aspires
to coffee. Day lily buds, crunchy,
sweet, dump—trust me—in soup.

For iron and calcium I enclose a field
of indestructible dandelion leaves. Toss
with a bouquet of orange nasturtiums—
or save those for a spicy sauce
that will make your insides dance
all the way back to shady maples
and me. To inflict a trance,

minty hot bee balm in tea. Lavender's
lemon zing. The violet's nectar, the pansy tart.
Carnation is cloves. The hollyhocks are bland
but sturdy. All over town
they're reinforcing wavering walls.

Live large—fling chrysanthemums
into your bowl of goat stew.

3. *Freshwater Amulets*

Here are sixteen pearly Buddhas
barely the size of my pinky nail.
That's sixteen peach-and-marble grins
(godawful know-it-alls) pearled
in an ancient mussel valve:
pre-Viking, pre-Hun, pre-Peloponnesian.
Stuck in that old "hurry up and wait?"
These Buddhas in your chest pocket
jostle the ammo and lip balm, shrug off
your restlessness. Caught between
this cryptic wall and that sly ditch?
All sixteen cross-legged amulets chuckle.
Please don't lend them too much
credence. In a quiet moment, when
a daydream poses little risk, imagine
a very soggy, very miniature, bottom-dwellers'
bowling match. Let each wobbly guru
stand for a pin. It's prudent,
so near the desert, to populate
a stream behind your eye.

4. Samurai Suit from the Edo Period

It won't protect you for long. In those days, warriors
were sent on parade. With each ceremonial bow, the chain-link
gauntlets and lamellar plating became prettier

and flimsier. Still, their helmets bore wings. Dragons
roared from their chests. The successful Samurai could stare for days
at a comatose ant. His garden bloomed and wept

identical yellow tears. He glowed in his lacquered face guard
like Harionna with barbed curls. Pouring tea into tiny cups,
he never spilt a drop or thought it possible. His killing

was equally precise. This is for the day you can't
blouse your pant legs over your boots one more time.
It comes with plates for shoulders, thighs, back, breast

and throat. Armoured gloves. When you can't abide one more
hour on a dirt floor. You dream your rifle rusted through, and wish
the grenade on the cool clay shelf by your cot was pure

decoration. Metal, doeskin, cotton, silk and horse-hair sprigs.
Double takes will ride the dust in your wake. No buried wires
will sizzle. No catches released, no barrels raised.

5. Things I've Stared at Since You Left

Five buzzing cubes of Spanish pyrite.
A humming handprint of San Diego elbaite.
The green velvet crooning of Arizonian malachite.
Breathless Sar E'Sang lazurite. The blue ache
of sea crystals trapped in white rock. The fog
in the quartz. The rose
in the quartz. Amethyst
pop-pop-pops. A black-and-violet
fluorite bruise. A Sicilian sulfur
desire, bright as a dish of lemon sorbet
on a stinking Roman patio. Guitar solos
of purple creedite. Calcite whites that witnessed,
through rings of grey, something ghastly
from the slope of the Harz Mountains.
Burnt Moroccan vanadinite from behind the brocade curtain,

under the occupied bed. The sweet caramel torture
of Tasmanian crocoite. A dusty heap
of Broken Hill anglesite. The scraped cavities
of Montana's Silver Star Mine. All the acid-tinted
glory of the Bronze Age, the blood and toil
of the Iron Age, compressed into rocks
a person might pick up and throw—
The bottom of Bunker Hill Mine, where the shavings lie.
The last glittery crumb of Idaho pyromorphite.
Gypsum that forewent its hold on the star.

6. Pep Talk from the Arctic Fox

The snowy owl blinked at me. I prowled her.
A short-tailed weasel slipped past me. I dug her.
The willow ptarmigan ruffled the branches. I ate her.
A white-throated sparrow serenaded me. I let her.

They played right in. That's what I mean
by sly. Not just to crouch unseen
between a dog-sled track and a mukluk.
I burrowed in wiles. I crept over luck.

When they emerge, throw on your whites.
Seal them in your sights—
whether pelting particles, cracked expanses.
(This is the part where you take no chances.)

My ear twitches: the ice floe is melting.
Would you give in by inches, go down sweltering?
Teeth bared, ears back, one paw midair,
freeze them in your tundra glare.

7. Tale of the Sable Antelope

Over foot-worn stairs, grooved horns
spiral a faint call to distant steppes.
Generations since the chase was lost, bare patches
shadow his jaw. Our brown-eyed savannah
beauty, eighty years in exile, ignores
that gorilla dangling by the window,
the lion on the move below the sill.

Four hooves touch the green weave,
a white chin lifts toward the blue
museum wall. Follow the horns arcing
toward that hint of a hump, up one flight
to the mummified cats (a little falcon too),
the upraised cobra and Hominin skulls,
that urn shaped like fat Uncle Sid.
Before you pass, listen:

back then, we traded in lives
like fine teas or plates. No sign
of the Bridled Gnu and Bleshok Ram,
his old companions. Did their legs, after
decades positioned just so, give way?
A hunt (the labs, the basement) might yield
remains. I'm trying to see in our trio
some lesson in diplomacy—

here, in this hush, expectations
roll like terriers in dirt. Friends
come and go. On the faraway plain
where the antelope fell, that mane
like night shot up.

8. *Instructions for Shrinking Your Enemy's Head*

Slit the scalp from crown to sloping
neck. The brain might bump
and squish. Press on: task
at hand. Pick a war, any

war. How many paused, cutters
raised, fists in mats of bloody hair?
The third soul, call him *Payback*—
ugh, call him Rank—slithered out,

polluting the fields. (Remember D-Day's
putrid fog?) Wriggle the skull
free. Sew lips and eyes fine. Boil
till reduced by two-thirds. Getting

there. OK. Stuff with hot
stones and hang above a well-stoked

fire overnight. Rest by the pulsing
embers. In the dewy morning,

polish the blackened face
with fire pit ash. That's it.
Foiled. The hissing, spitting
force is sealed.

9. *World-famous Photographer, Robert Polidori*

When he's lining up his shot, step away from your cot.
Before him, not a snag in a discarded bathrobe is safe,
not even the 16th-Century stench in the blur of tapestries

at Versailles. On his knees in the Samir Geagea Headquarters
in Beirut, sleeves scrunched at his elbows, he plunged
into charred files. He stooped through a blown-out

wall, helicoptered over sandbags, and listened. The light
on the slack, knotted burlap sang to him of something pink
and sore, smeared over the doorframe. The song was

nails in his ears. In Havana, where jail cells reverberate
with scratching pens, he snuck into the Señora Faxas Residence.
Beneath exposed ceiling slats, he revealed a single book

(atop hundreds more). At the Teatro Capitalio, an orange
fright spread over chunks of plaster. Revolutions
were peeling off the balconies. In his fist, which closes

over many bits and bobs, you might spot a length
of wire, still twitching, from the Control Room of Reactor 4—
or four gangly cribs (long relieved of their swaddled

occupants) from the Exclusion Zone maternity ward,
titptoeing out of Pripyat. Down south, New Orleans
saddled him with drowned wardrobes in twin closets;

a nose-diving sedan, its back bumper snagged
on an eavestrough; a four-poster wrangled from the ocean's
jaws, its quilt a volcanic beach. The atmosphere

roils. Polidori's quit sleep. When he waves down

your LAV, consider the dry sunrise, the clay
hollows, the missteps marking every path

outside the compound. This pitter-patter
bombing on and on—this assassination weather
—these igniting bureaucracies—this warlord

arm-wrestle—blackmail crops—amnesty wheels—
they're just disturbances he means to trick
into his little round lens. Shoulder your kit.

His viewfinder hovers. Hold out
your hand-me-down grenade, your bandana
and sleeves of instant coffee. Call it a trade.

10. Ziplock Baggie of Seahorse Specimens

Shake it before a patch of light:
one dwarf, one lined, one slender.
The new Caledonian, the Eastern Pacific,
and—careful, she's tumbled to a corner—
Hippocampus Denise, the smallest of the small,
stretching one full centimetre from her Cyrano de Bergerac
snout, over her lumpy coronet, down the bony
plates (two knobs and a spine at each
junction), through the jovial
tail, in, in,
in. The museum owns
3,000. The curators carry them about
just this way—in sandwich bags—
to show off to tourists. They're dry; try
not to crush them. A team of such creatures
drew Poseidon's chariot through the depths.

Invisible in seagrass, they bounce
over sponges, pilings and weeds—
pick one—latch on. Yank and pull, they won't
let go, they'd sooner let a current drop them
three oceans away. They digest whole
crustaceans by magic (no stomach, no teeth).
They transport water fairies and cure the worst
ailments (leprosy, infertility). In 1990, in writing,
a scientist confessed, "Seahorses are so

unusual that it can be difficult to accept
that they are fishes." Right. I forgot.
Aside from all this, they are fishes.

Complicated seahorse courtship: the male turns
bright orange, the female pink. They rise belly-to-belly
from the seabed, grasp at a willowy stalk, and pivot
like carousel ponies. Everyone goes on about   .
the male and his ingenious pouch: he
incubates the babies. One enthusiastic specimen
bore a brood of 1,572. (If you ask me, he overdid it.)
But after all those strange fish wriggled to the surface,
gulped and zoomed off, mom and dad
resumed their breakfast waltz, dorsal fins trembling
over curly-q tails. My fondness for these creatures
distracts me. I stumble after waking to the kitchen,
uncap the marker, approach the wall, "X"
one box. I'd swim way, way down
for such intimate circlings
and gentle greetings.

from Cottonopolis:

Tablecloth

In coffles they come, coughing, onto sloops, schooners, brigs, snows. On houses with wings! On snows! In Liverpool, snow falls on snows; in Manchester, it falls into the river Irk, onto chilblained Hands.

At the Castle, Governors Mould and Corps drink punch. The jungle encroaches. By next midwinter, the road will be gone again. And look at this cloth. White muslin, some fancy flower in the centre. A lily perhaps? What once were folds are now just holes, holes and holes. Below them, the table, stockings crawling with ants, the slave-hole. Above, a blue sky. Vultures on guns honeycombed with rust rise up to shriek their greetings. Hello, Hello. Here come the snows.

Jar

This is, after all, a new world. Iron brands, bands laid across meadow, fallow field. They say cow's milk'll turn sour at the sound. They say the speed will crush your lungs. They say you could lie a sleeper line of mangled legs along this track. Wheels turn, the hare flees, rain falls in sheets. Over a hundred bales of cotton in her sides. We left Liverpool this morning. Some years back, there were signs in her windows: Silver Locks and Collars for Blacks and Dogs.

We'll reach Cottonopolis next. The train's greased with palm oil. See it shine.

The gun goes off. Scramble!! Bodies shine. Slaves run, fling themselves overboard and are seized again. And later, we'll take this palm oil, this gold in a glass, and spread it on our trains and on our bread for tea.

Cask

Scow-bankers, beach horners, wharfingers: they haunt every port, brown-gummed and blind, spewing black blood. Bruises splotches of ink on grey paper. Gone the mouth, gone the legs, gone the sunburnt nose. Walk down this green road. I'll know thee by thine eyes.

The fog horn blows. Mersey Men unload barrels, shovel sugar, heave cotton bales. And in Bridgetown, Kingston, Roseau, sailors shiver and sweat. They huddle under derricks, hands curled over rotting toes. Crawl into this empty cask, sugar grit against the skin.

Everything is green here. Sweet sop trees, hibiscus for your true love's hair. The fog lifts. Heave away boys, heave away.

Muslin Dress

So here are lines of torn trees, dragged out by the roots. Lines of Redmen and squaws, curved line of babies on backs. Ragged line of footprints in snow.

Coffle line of Negroes, sent to clear land then fill it. Line of cotton in the field. Line of the lash. Twenty-five if the line of a leaf makes its way into the clouds of cotton. Twenty-five if the line of a branch is broken in the field.

There's that straight line the gun makes, the angle made with the torso when the arm is stretched out. The lines in the slave pen. The lines their fingers make as he moves them back and forth, to see if they'll pick cotton.

Here are the railway lines and there are the shipping lines. Here's the factory line. The line of children in the mines. The chimney lines. There is the line: from the cotton gin to the Indian.

The lines you've memorized, the lines of your white muslin dress, the way it falls in folds to the ground. All eyes are on you. For a moment, it's as if all lines stop here.

Photograph, Negro

And ye shall know them by their fruits. The small lumps on his back, a bunch of grapes. Or this Negro's blackberry bramble! Raspberry, honeysuckle, rose. Head turned away. Hand on hip.

Crab-apples, dewberries, pine-apples, blackberries. Come by! Come by! The crops are in. Grapes shot—volleyed in the humid air. Ladies croquet, shuttlecock on silent lawns.

Do men gather grapes of thorns? Across the sea, bog cotton, purple heather, bees in clover. Upland cotton in airless rooms. Factory hands have arms and we have cut his off. We've made honey from the marrow of his bones.

The Scarborough Bluffs

You will not find me among the women of the earth,
Their hair wound up in buns upon their heads,
And goosebumped legs bridged above the bath—

I am not with them. But let it not be said
That an Orpheus doesn't sound them
That behind me suddenly he isn't

Eurydice, his the face to which I may not
Turn and look, or else,
As prayers of rescue rise to no messiah.

Decades later and a block away
The Alzheimer takes off her glasses and her coat
And half-naked amid the snow she lays

In the cedar-ribbed hull of a boat
On neighbourless Lake Gibson, June, as five
Stone blocks of thought leopard the lakebed.

And all alone tonight I'll drive
These empty streets
And for the first time in forever feel alive,

Feel the secular roar of the Gardiner,
And smile at how in the land of the nightmask
Mascara is a kind of queenmaker.

I leave the zoo with the moon on the park,
The wolves asleep, the lions going down
(even the sun leaves Scarborough before it's dark)

And the lot of us descend to the Bluffs,
The keloid scar where a wound has frescoed
Over the vanishing land's gag order to the south.

A figure in the varves emerges like Francesca
From Rodin's *Gates of Hell*. We discandy from the stone,
Paolo and me, split a sweating Fresca

And walk the eyeless avenues alone.

Cradle and light

The cradle of the train rocking through the dusk.
I am going to see my father who has had a stroke.
Dirty rows of corn zipper past, and the white roofs
of farms hover over fields in the weakening light.
Solitary trees stand crooked over empires of bales
faltering to ash. In the August heat this ripened landscape

is like an image in a still pond. Inside the train
children pass back and forth in the aisle. Something
about them seems to slow the light, make the day
linger and resist the shadows seeping in from the fields.
Maybe it's the laughter or the whimsical screaming,
but even they can't make it stop, and soon the train

is lit from within. I can see its glow flickering past
on the ground in the dark beside the sway-and-rap
of axles and wheels. And now, the children have stilled.
The faces of their parents are bent on seats,
even they glow a little, the air filmy with their sleep.
The train is like a moon gliding past farmhouses

in the dark, a memory of laughter that briefly
held the light—its cargo the uneasy dreams dreamed
between the places we must get to, and leave.

Small Story

So the tree. And the wrongful
way the wind de-leaved it.
Down to bare bark and skid-wracked
branches. But I'm exaggerating of course.
This is the law of all taking. Savour the small moments—
apples with their red out, skins glossed to luster.

Hamlet

Houses by highways
Lunches by lamp,
Hamlet in highschools
hamlets and camps.

Hamlet the hero
Hamlet himselves,
Hamlet hermetic
high up on shelves.

Hamlet in Heorot
goldfish on hooks
Hamlet in whoredens,
hookers with books.

Hamlet in headphones
henhouses, huts,
Harvard and Hellmans'
hamsamwiches,

nuts. Historical
Hamnet, Hamlet
the Man. Heaven for
children, Hamlet

Japan. Horses for
Hamlet, Hamlet in
hooves, Yahoos for Ham—
let, Hot Cat Tin Roofs.

Why hello there Hamlet,
horrible friend,
Happy to see you,
how have you been?

"Hungry and harrow,
Hamburg to Hoth,
slings arrows vengeance
then am I off

"To houses by high—
ways, highschools and
homes, Lunches by lamp
light, Russia to

Rome". Oh Hooray, poor
Hamlet, homeless
and old. Prince of mankind,
Helvetica

bold.

Don Draper

Moths feather your far gazebo
like young sailors on first leave.
You know something, and keep reminding me

of my own needs. You see an audience
of blooming heads and sugared bank notes,
and act accordingly. The swallows see it at five o'clock,

a Wolfman's tragedy.
They hang themselves upside down,
handsome sienna prizes in the semaphore of bats.

Swayed by a summer night, I swing out
to your silk pocket square standing at attention,
a bird about-face. You're the dark dew on the green grass of home.

Katahdin

Why couldn't I love him? He was all good morning
beautiful and you deserve to be spoiled, bringing me coffee
in bed, balancing the cups in that prissy way. Why couldn't
I ignore that? His air of resignation, slumped behind the wheel,
always just under the speed limit, docile yes officer at the border.
Nothing on him to give those in authority what they want.
To my, this isn't going anywhere, he said, well, I like what I see.
His respect for social order, corporations, the business section.
Not rights, but responsibilities. His regret for the years I spent
smoking dope. A whiz with engines, quadratics, but not overly
analytical. Something about beer, pizza and women, he said.
And mountains, escorting me to the top of Katahdin, a mile
high, on a lucent autumn day, a small Gore-Texed crowd
dazzled at the summit, taking in Chimney Pond, the knife
edge. But all I wanted to do was get back down.

Unisphere at Midnight, Flushing Meadows, NY. 1981

I have fallen through the earth and onto concrete.
A death mask, lifted off the life of the World
of Tomorrow. I can see stars behind it. I am dying
in the past tense, in the reflecting pool of dying.
I consider my republic: that of stupid men who faltered
on drunken Arctic expeditions. We slipped on grime,
on Greenland. I slipped on fizzled history, the
failed lights behind old capitols. I crashed against
the futuristic blitz of metric timing. I fell for microdays.
I fell for US Steel, the imperial aesthetic. I bashed
my head on the equator and bled a slick for UNICEF.
I died, democratic. The sirens I inspired have all been
turned away. The steel pings a moment and then forgets
my head. It's a small world. I stood above it, after all.

What was that poem?

My mother asked me, What was that poem?
It was Longfellow's "My Lost Youth," I think.
The answer was Longfellow, often enough,
even though she never liked Evangeline.

I talked to my mother on my cellphone
outside a grocery store in Philadelphia.
She asked me what I was buying, *Was it dear?*,
and if I now liked football more than baseball.

It was the last conversation I ever had with her.
I told her I liked baseball, to make her happy.
I knew she wasn't calling to talk sports.
She was showing off, saying, "I'm going to be okay!"

What was that poem? she'd say and act surprised
when I didn't know. It wasn't about the answer.
It was about noticing something held on to,
with wit and ferocity, until the day is done.

Belfast

Pour me a bit of something to drink, and leave
it sitting on the counter until I get home—
I've got your pictures here to look at when
forgetting we're happy, for when the bonfires

light the underside of the clouds, when old
ladies yell into the phones their children
insisted they have, when the whiskey bonder
becomes the spirit merchant becomes the barman.

Served and reserved, I'm getten—move on down
the line. Crane works unwinding, lifting
mostly air these days. They all look you straight
in the ear, past the shoulder's escape route.

Nobody's really here anymore, are they?
Friday nights empty of recognition,
except where women are helped home, fags lit,
barefoot with sandals dangling from a finger.

Ashes on TV, the river buried
below, a pipe under all neighbourhoods—
water's tangled hair straightened with a comb
into Brylcreemed rows of marching men.

Buses between streets, the population on
permanent inhale—short sucks of heaven
accumulate in the lungs, overcrowded
prisons, or each breath the clock needs for a tick.

Spare a moment for the buried mothers,
even if you're not the crying kind—
there's all this anger pointed at nothing,
a day's bad mood carried into the blood.

Background Noise

Home, my coat just off, the back room
murky and still, like the side altar of a church, so at first

I don't know what I hear:
one low, sustained, electronic note

keening seamlessly across my ear. I spot
the glow of the stereo, left on all morning,

the CD arrested since its final track, just empty signal now,
an electro-magnetic aria of frequency backed

by the wall clock's whirr, the dryer snoring in the basement,
wind, a lawnmower, the rev and hum of rush hour

returning on the parkway. I hit the panel's power button,
pull the plug on clock and fridge, throw some switches,

trip a breaker, position fluorescent cones to stop the traffic.
But still that singing at the edge of things.

I cut down overhead power lines, bleed the radiator dry,
lower flags, strangle the cat

so nothing buzzes, knocks, snaps or cries.
Then I shut the factories, ban

mass gatherings, building projects and road work,
any hobbies that require scissors, shears, knitting needles, cheers,

chopping blocks, drums, or power saws. It's not enough.
I staple streets with rows of egg cartons. I close

the airports, protest the use of wind farms, lobby
for cotton wool to be installed on every coast. No luck.

I build a six-metre wide horn-shaped antenna, climb
the gantry to the control tower, and listen in.

I pick up eras of news reports, Motown, Vera Lynn, Hockey
Night in Canada, so attempt to eliminate all interference,

pulsing heat or cooing pigeons, and there it is:
that bass, uniform, residual hum from all directions,

no single radio source but what I'm told is resonance
left over from the beginning of the universe. Does it mean

I'm getting closer or further away? It helps to know
what bounds there are, whether we're particle, wave or string,

if time and distance expand or circle, which is why
I need to learn to listen, even while I'm listening.

Some Birds

1

Observe that heron's hyperbolic stride,
the sinister way in which it seems to glide
on underwater rollerblades until
it halts and leans to peep across the sill
of the cattails and hypodermics its kill—
speared bullfrog or a bream. The great blue
is terrible and righteous when it pierces,
a marshy critic with a malice-javelin
deflating the fat white bellies of its catch.
I loath, yet am infatuated with, that heron.

2

The gallinules will shame me for my ponderous
approach to life. They have a buoyant levity
as they paddle plumply on the rank canal.
I hope to apply against my debacles
their aqueous placidity. Their horned feet
trundle the muddy depths to keep afloat.

3

Anhinga rookeries with their
brash, almost crackly chatter
set my arm-hairs on edge and give me
the gags, —that putrescent glitter
of fish-skin against gray twig,
under the leisurely parade of
self-important cumulus, leaves a
tufted taste in the mouth.

4

The Secretary Bird
(Sagittarius serpentarius)

When the secretary bird
appears in procession on the sandy veldt
of its "natural enclosure" at the zoo,
I tremble to my toes.
The secretary bird's a pacer.
It has quills
jutting backwards like a bookkeeper's Bic,
a fierce comptroller's
beak which it employs

to run its victims through.
It stabs them punctually
dotting each iota with its nib.

But I have witnessed it
—Bozo and Baryshnikov—
rotate beak-over-claws in air.
I applaud its bravura, its
panache. I love its grave
parade, its almost episcopal
gravitas, archimandrate
addicted to somersaults.

5
Birds are my nerves, my nervousness,
my metabolic tendrils to the world.

Range

Bulbous, chromed like a Fifties car;
fifty years old, like the house;
only one burner still lit—
even unwatched pots wouldn't boil.
Offhand advice said junk it.
But not our friend Klaus.

Clanking, he leapt from his truck,
cranked the stove's snowy hood;
peered into glass-fuse orbs.
Gingerroot thumbs nudged coils.
With falcon-beak pliers, he stirred
black-lava reaches of crud,

knit frizzing wire. He eased
the range sideways, humming;
draped copper around new bolts,
strands over a child's ear;
tapped; squinted; hovered—
ruddying, a quartet of suns.

Klaus shook his head at our cheque,
scooped tools, patted the stove's
chipped door. "Bake me two stollen."
With your double labor of love
you will have given us hundreds,
and all you ask is two loaves.

Bear Room

His bears were several, my grandfather's:
two big grizzlies, a small black bear,
one on the floor and two on the wall,
with heads on hassocks. Moose antlers,
hide. A wolf, a lynx, a chamois,
something else I cannot name,

deer family. A furry basement room,
big fireplace, dimmer switch, green bulb
transplanted and weird. Little, I worked the bellows,
endlessly changed the light. Inherited, in time,
the lynx, the chamois head, even the rifles.
They came to us in my late teens, in boxes,

like all mythic death waiting under wraps,
the Bear Room vestigial. As a child in that room,
though the oldest, I was the most afraid,
the finest fear when lit. Such a second retina I had
as a muskox has, animating forms in green light:
a live and luminous animalia, phosphorescent, angry.

Wretched with love on the day Opa died,
I worked this exposure: I brought a friend to the
Bear Room, and when it stopped him cold,
I lost that clarifying eye, those figures.
("Have you ever been downstairs in this house?")
"My God," he whispered, looking around.

"I know," I said, and my voice wigged out
like any living thing's caught by the scruff.

Paperweight

I bought it, I admit, because the thing has clout,
looks tough—like what a serious person does with paper.
All forged in brass or bronze or metal clods, it's a buffalo
ranging over vinyl plains under clear skies of polyurethane:
shaggy head, ballerina haunch, it looks half
starved as if it foraged on the plastic junk
caught on a barbed wire fence which it kind of is,
I guess, laid across the open range of my desk.
Glossy. Cold. A bit slippery to the touch
like the photos of extinct herds at Head Smashed In Buffalo Jump,
when it falls—it must weigh a quarter pound—
on solid oak, look how it leaves a mark!
I got it years ago in Winnipeg (see, below
the galloping legs, the knollish "n"s,
the roman font) though I didn't even know, then,
where buffalo paperweights were supposed to go—
I still can't imagine what hurricane or blout
I'd need to justify its mass and then, if so,
would just one be enough? Now, as I get this out,
I think it's about as good at keeping paper down
as ink on 20-lb stock—that heavy black or red
(saved for Jesus and bankers) holding it all together,
an anchor for the eye as it sails, head on, toward that everpresent whiteout:
Snow blind. Searchlight. Whitest white.
Paper's barely even there, no wonder
it needs a weight. Or here. Tell you what,
I doubt this ink's enough: go ahead,
tear this page out.

Scene

(for Ted Byrne)

Nothing happens for the first time
    it likes what I said

it increases in speed like a train
    because newness is possible

I was eating apricots on the train
    with the sense of a relay

as the blunt monuments of the nuclear reactors
    rose from a refulgent landscape

or l'èxces, l'audace, la marge et l'érudition
    in the images of Poussin

I continued in the presence of fear
    to try to think about the spaciousness of poetry

I brought the horror of the political economy into my body
    and this became a style

but I escaped from most things
    at uncertain intervals and unsuitable times

words, the eye, bodies, tall ships, scoured plains, huge forests
    perhaps they flank the subject

like porous baffles that refract
    every organ's part in living

to seek the indifferent order
    of a childhood

a field slowly regurgitates its stone
    it is then heaped at some half-hidden site at the edge

from which clandestinely grows
    buttressed by rusted scrap and gorse

a lanky wild cherry tree
    beneath it I stand, spitting seed

I eat the over-ripe, splitting-open fruit from the ground
    as would any animal

in June here the fox turds are clotted
    with pale cherry pips

it is the field's slow work to produce such turd
    from stone

thinking is this hesitant
    I keep pushing colour into it and then I sand it off

what I love is pleached
    the day retreats from the present

the movement, just outside perception
    traverses limbs, skin, organs, hair

as if it were the meaning of this sentiment
    not to be expressed

the extent to which this meaning does not exist
    ripens

there's a whirring of birds over mustard
    their wings are troubling the pods

with irony and tenderness
    like it wrinkles, puckers, near a scar

the image is not optical
    the same for beauty

I was using my own body
    as a needle

to play out an idea about beginning
    as a practical, portable gift

when a bell rang three times, behind it
    the river and massing of boughs

a young girl is by herself in a yard
    throwing darts

she fiercely flings her weapons
    at very close range to the target

reaches forward to collect the darts
    then throws them again

she repeats the ritual three times in all
    (it is late afternoon in the village)

then she retrieves her cane from the long grass
    limps slowly to the house

I feel a deep identification
    with the sullen awkward girl

who seems not to have chosen
    her own oddly flounced skirt

the spirituality of the present
    cheats in its yard

and is unlegislated
    ideology

savage with gravitas
    whose mystic target collapsed

tottering with the load
    like a fratricide ballad

all stomp and clap
    and esoteric cruelty

an apple tree
    clotted with mistletoe

seen from
    a train.

Academic Liaison

The mathematics of her ultimate failure had

something to do with her curves, an errant root;
  nothing to do with reason, rules or hyperbolic paraboloids.
Something to do, she thinks, with set facts.

Nothing to do with *his* drilling dry exercise—
  It's the way *he* demands that she try harder at home,
study *his* mastery, subtract herself from the equation.

When it becomes the way a young man bears weight
  into the classroom and angles it on the desk before her,
it seems even youth can worship weathered physics—

and desire is a test she might work her way through.
  Nothing to do with calculation at all.
Something to do with a void filled.

It's thrust and yield, the unfluctuating support in a point.
  It's studied distance, the lengths she might go to.
Nothing to do with figures, but relations factor.

Something to do with this man, at twenty plus two,
  oh—yes, it seems a fraction of an answer carried over,
and the altered shape of her has something – no,

everything to do with the pure balance of one on one.

Lift Up Your Eyes

It's dark by five. The time
of year we cleave to lightboxes, their travel
versions, and dawn simulators ordered online
from the SAD Light Superstore. West, there is some
daylight left, and later, by the North's lantern, its plains
are read in black, white, grey, and lighter
grey, a beauty acknowledged in the animal way
with the whole mind, in a strategy. Distance
lies heavily on that municipality, its roads,
as will the snow, and more so now the school has
gone, and the store, closure of which inaugurated
the season and its proprietors' bankruptcy. Neighbours
rallied to help keep their electricity on, but when even this
could no longer be done, they moved in
with family in another town. He'd been back to gather
a few last things—people had seen him there—
returned to his daughter's home and died of
heart attack that afternoon. I met him once or twice,
it being years since I've lived in that place,
which like all others is unlike any in the details
of its luck and failures. We hate the one to whom
we belong, and love the one we don't. Winter will say
its long mass over him, over troubled ground upon which
are written the liturgies, the ends of the earth. Anything
going has far to go. As they wandered. I heard the news
on the phone. They'd come from the east coast.

Blues

Toot me something on your golden horn
he said to the musician.
I feel cold as my soul turns blue.

Jerryrig me an intricate song
full of those diminished sevenths
and just enough thrust to push me through

bar by smoky bar, into oblivion.
Extricate me for thorny feelings,
Put brain and heart to sleep.

Bring out a flute and its Bolivian
so sorrow can be trumped by sorrow.
Afford me, at any price, some peace.

Today I am bedeviled
befogged by this predictment:
will I find myself myself again tomorrw?

A Wind-Aided Fire

Pretend it's eight o'clock again.
No one's dictating anything—
the little cassettes sit stacked in their cases.
Forget about the boxes of bullets
above the bed in the cabin's spare bedroom,

forget about those hunting parties
that used to push off from the mooring mast
in the prototypes for the flaccid dirigible—

those burgeoning balloonists
and their pulleys and ramps and the little men on bikes
who race around the gondola… And if you can, act
like we're in the cold desert

—among nose cones and tail sections;
pieces for steering, the skeletons of wings.

Re-envision the commodore.
Appreciate his loyalty to hangers-on; the polishing
of the screw until it's the very curve
of resentment.

Luxuriate in how this all started with clowns.
Clowns and seltzer and tears—

    maybe it all started with the tears?
The tears were definitely there first,
like snail silk in the *a priori* blackness,
spooky and silent as an unplugged theremin.

Sometimes it's just too easy to put it all together
like this. Take note of some things:

the mass exodus of clowns under cover
of a wind-aided fire;
those museums in Mexico
where the cholera mannequins stand around
like ramshackle victims;

the black tape, the black boxes, the spinning,
and the game you want to learn
so you can be found dead playing it;

the black outlines
of antennas backlit by the city;
the low lake levels
and the emerging snarl of shopping carts—

and then the wind.

See them on the move:
   armed with blackjacks and wigs
and false moustaches—
foreign and uncertain and conscious
of their nudity
in the halls of the neighbourhoods.

But patience—
       patience
and the constancy of storm fronts.

Patience and the palm-bitten nails.
     Patience and the water-borne illness.
         Patience and the lung-engulfing plague.

We can all laugh.
We can all make casts of each other's
most private places. We can whip ourselves

with the lash of the deafening possible,
and pretend it's still a couple of hours ago.

After riding the escalator back

to switch the watch
a Swatch a second time, a third,
each face scratched minutely,

or because the date was stuck
I became a traveller in the mall
forever unhappy with a purchase

but returning always unalone
brought there with my wife
who loves me and worries for

the sorrow that ticks away
inside the case of my self-schism
but that's not all

I go up and offer each broken
or semi-imperfect object to
the kindly merchant of watches

who resembles a small Paul Simon
which is smaller than you might
imagine possible, and while

outside there is London getting
Sunday under a darkening wing
inside it is the timelessness

of some brief caring act,
not entirely due to exchange of
money, and I am in love

and ruined in some parts of inner
workings, a cog that clicks
upon another toothed gear

stymied again, under the magnifying
glass, still unable to be pried free—
sorrow's just an hour by hour

journey, but in between, there are
seconds as good as before, pretty
good intervals to cling to you and me.

Little Animals

On bokes for to rede I me delyt.

1

That old book has a million moving parts,
and when you open it to look inside,
they all spill out, like the escapement
from a sproinged clock,
spelling up the life and correspondence
of a Dutch cloth merchant called van Leeuwenhoek.
A regular little factory, this book,
as busy as a Jacquard loom
constructing its bustling world
of high-piled clouds and shambling
courtyards and canals,
and copper gutters filling up with rain,
a 17th-century rain, curled
like a great cascading periwig
over the cankered rooftiles of old Delft.

It has some chickens in it, and a hive of bees
and 16 coffin-bearers and a bowl,
(and divers things too numerous to name).
Press your eye against the page
and marvel at the makes that shift
this pretty engine, with its
weights and wormscrews,
tumbling cams and pins,
all shaped by hand & cunningly contrived
to move a miniature Dutchman through his life.

2

He was the first Microscopist,
a worldly man compelled
by wasteful curiosity to build
a homely magnifier and enlarge
inconsequential items: fishscales,
pepper, fly-stings, dandruff, dust,
nose hair, spidersilk, some stuff
he found between his teeth,
and he was the first to do a thing
the finest intellects of Europe never thought of,
which was to look, to simply look,
inside a water drop

at all the thrashing whiptailed swimmers,
motile cogs and quaking ghosts
that make their lives in there,
and these he called his "little animals,"
some appearing in the glass
"as large as your arm" and others,
"as small as the beard hairs of a man
that hath not in a fortnight shaved,"
disporting themselves with merry
convolutions, flexing their numerous
limbs and nimble paws
in a manner pleasing to a haberdasher's eye,
commendatory to the Genius
of their Maker.

3

So, here was a man who looked
at pieces of his world and found
more worlds inside them,
which is the natural order: worlds
that roost in tiny apertures on worlds
where dainty worldlings
dwell, and each one
is a world as well, some
milling in the streets of Delft and others,
pulsing through pondwater.
And each of these should have a book.
And there should be a book
for every punctuation mark
in all those books, and every speck
should be recorded and preserved
so that all things in time might be
made known and magnified
and put before us in the book of books.

But for now there is only this excellent one
by Clifford Dobell to enjoy,
and I have neglected to mention
the best part, which is the bookplate pasted
on its inside cover, ornately framed
in the Art Nouveau style,
and the picture inside it
which hangs in a well-lit stillness,

calm and perplexing as a tarot card,
over a rippling armorial ribbon
bearing a line from Chaucer.

It is a scene from mythical Arcadia, not
the prefecture of modern Greece,
but the literary, made-up place
where idle minds imagine
poetry belongs: sloping pastures
on unpopulated hills,
a billowing meringue of clouds
stitched with careful penstrokes,
a lonely place, at once
intimate and remote, for this
is a *private* wilderness, a place
for nobody to find but me,
and curled up at the bottom
of a vine-laden sycamore sits
a boyish short-horned faun, his hooves
tucked up beneath him, and instead
of scamping through purple freshets,
"trilling joyously on oaten pipe,"
or humping dryads, as it may be,
in a dappled grove,
the little goat is captivated by
a book too small to read the title of,
and look how he holds it, his book,
exactly as I hold mine, his head
a little tilted, one hand propping up his chin,
the picture of perfect absorption,
a picture of life at its best,
because, what else is there to do
in Paradise but loaf beneath a tree,
and dream of other worlds?

4

Or peer for hours and hours,
and more hours adding up to years,
through bits of polished glass
at beings who have no idea
they are being watched?

5

A spring rain pools on the porch-chairs
at the group home for addicts,
and the same rain soaks a toddler's sock
that has been lying in my yard all year
and this is the very rain
that fills a frog pond down the road
where I go to collect little animals
to look at in my microscope.
It is all I have done this week.
I am neglecting my life
to spy on theirs! And if I had a shop that sold
button loops and red kersey
and bombazine at 9 stivers an ell,
that shop would surely fail,
with no one there to watch the till,
for you would find me locked upstairs instead
in a rambling sun-stunned room,
the room where Vermeer himself
might well have painted
our hero in his scholar's robe, with his
star globe and dividers
and his cabinet of handmade
brass and silver microscopes, a man
of his time, staring until the light ran out at things
not mentioned in the Bible.

And I am a man of my time, but my
microscope came here from China
in a foam box reeking of solvents,
and the first live thing I saw in it
was a piece of myself, a tiny monster
from the back of my tongue: a macrophage,
whose role in my life is to eat
my enemies, the black
jots and whits, the lithe and vibrating
umlauts, hyphens & tildes that would use me for food—
and that is where you will find Narcissus
today, gazing down at himself
on a clean glass slide,
on which a nano-assassin
encapsulated in a see-through sphere
is taking care of business, and there

in its scintillant middle I could see
my would-be devourers
being devoured, a pleasing sight.
And the next thing I looked at was yogurt.
And then, I walked out to the pond.

6

On the path to the pond
there's a hole, fairly large,
where a pope-faced turtle old enough
to be my grandmother buried her eggs
last year. It is littered with leathery
shells and I have a strong urge
to fill up my pockets with these,
but it is not what I came for. The place
where I gather my samples
reminds me of a ruined Roman
amphitheatre, there are trees all around it
frozen in gestures of theatrical
menace and operatic grief.
A private wilderness, but the air here
is not quiet, it is shrill with sex,
the unceasing, imperious, loud need
of these treefrogs insisting on sex.
There is skim-ice on the water,
still, and there are animals under there, too,
demanding sex, and in truth
I would not refuse it myself,
if some girl with a high forehead
rinsed in the silvery light of old Delft
were to stop pouring milk
or reading her mail
and come out to the musky woods
where a goat-footed stranger is waiting.
But now, I must open a hole in the ice
with my long-handled spoon
and scoop out a helping of murk
to fill my bowl.

7

It is water, the restless stuff
that sustains and dissolves us,
and I tell you, though you will never

believe what I say, it is alive inside,
for there are animals within it
smaller even than the mites
upon the rind of a cheese,
"and their motions in water
are so swift and various,
upwards, downwards, and round about
that it is wonderful to see."
For it is down in the grey
and mazy darkness of the pond
that they are constructing their
glittering clattertrap City of Madness,
with its glass ladders, and lemon-green
spirals and a sky traversed by
delirious weirdos, one
like an angry emoticon, with two long hairs
embrangled on its scalp,
one like a revolving cocklebur,
and another like an animated spill,
(as if an accident could live!)
and crescent moons and popeyed gorgons, things
with knives for hands,
frenetic writhers, tumblers, bells
on stalks, a sort of great loose
muscle flinching and contracting,
diatoms like crystalline
canoes serenely gliding
down a coast of brown decay, and suddenly,
what looks to be a throbbing bronze
Victrola trumpet
rocketing around as if it won the war!
And you can almost hear the fanfare
as it plants its small end in a clump of muck
and starts to stretch itself,
and stretch until it is
as long as an alp horn,
as long and quivering as a plume of smoke
as long and quivering and dreadful as a cyclone funnel,
working the furious hairs of its mouth to suck
its lessers down its throat.

8

I have stared at them all week
in my Chinese microscope and have tried
to absorb what I saw.
I have studied my little animals so closely,
and have memorized their names,
the names they received
from muttonchopped scholars in the age
of tailcoats and columnar hats, there was
lacrymaria olor, tears
of the swan, by which we mean
that it is somewhat tear-shaped, if a tear
should have a long prehensile neck
to wrap around its food,
and there was *stentor* the loudspeaker,
which speaks for itself,
rotaria rotatoria,named
for the whirling cartwheels on its mouth,
suctoria, because it sucks, *amoeba*
because it makes me sick,
digenea because, merciful God,
I have never seen anything like that,
and *paramecium* which slides
like a long grey shadow
through a world it knows by feel,
serene as a basking shark,
and takes what it needs
and gives nothing.

And there is no end to them,
no end in numbers,
and no end in strangeness,
no end to their appetites, and all of it
exactly as van Leeuwenhoek
described it to us all those years ago,
when he, being the first to *look*
became the first to see
that what the wise men said was wrong,
what gnaws at our lapsed and sinful
world is not death at all,
the old machinework mannequin
swinging his scythe, he is not there.
It is not Death that undresses us,

pulls at the loose threads,
teases our garments apart,
and thrusts itself down
to make more of itself inside us,
nor is it Death
that incises those lines
in our cheeks
and lays his corrupting touch
on a Dutch girl's breast,
or calls up to us
from the cool earth
under the ice-covered pond—

for if you look, simply look,
with your bit of ground glass
you will see what is eating
these holes in the world, what chews
at the black straggle
and clings to those rafts of algae,
and cries up from the pages of a
strange old book, and hangs
in the damp sycamores
hollering for sex, sex, sex,
and probes in the dark muck
with its snakelike head,
if that thing is its head,
then opens its sudden mouth
with its wheel of whirling hairs
and starts to pull one
world after another
into its throat.

Brothers

One spent nights on the junior high school roof.
My mother had kicked him out when the police told her
he was selling drugs, and before that, selling tires
he stole from gas stations. One stole a teacher's car
from the senior high school parking lot at lunch time,
got a case of beer, and drove around drunk all afternoon,
then smashed the car's front fender when he re-parked it.
One threw a Molotov cocktail into a teacher's home
when the teacher accused him of copying an essay.
The same one beat up his P.E. teacher. One beat up
the leader of a gang. With that gang after him,
he started his own gang, he himself its only member,
and wore a red bandana and red old lady's jacket
to school every day. No one along the gauntlet
that had been set up to stop him touched him.
Each one headed to "alternate school." A year or two,
and the school was the bar, the drunk tank, jail.
But each one changed, and turned himself around.
Here we all are, suddenly in our mid and late thirties,
with everyone fooled. Clean-living, clean-looking,
all of us successful, and good middle-class boys.
One a CEO, one a president of marketing... all
with pretty partners, nice cars, nice paid-for houses.
And smilers and jokers around a dinner table.
Until something comes out after a beer or glass of wine
too many, a note in a voice, and we are all there in a row
and looking to either side of ourselves at each other,
trying to see the thing looking out of our faces
as out of cold, dark trees it stands at the edge of
and blends in with, each of us knowing it is there,
each of us ready to kill it, even when we know it is one of us,
though none of us knows which of us it is, only
that it is there and it is a lone, long-absent animal,
starving and afraid and ready to kill, and our father.

Common Loon
Gavia immer

All bird guides begin with 'loon.'
You are most ancient, most prehistoric,

as all can attest who hear your call
oscillate across a dark lake, quirky as a quasar,

harking back to a time before humans
began to gawk at the night sky

(star-spangled like your back) and wonder,
whence all this cosmic commotion?

You are the spirit in the shaking tent,
the belief in an abiding mystery,

something alive in the mute cosmos
besides our nattering selves. A voice

that vibrates in the reptilian brain, echoing
an old word we once knew, need more than ever.

Killdeer
Charadrius vociferus

You might chide your mother for her seeming carelessness,
the shallow scrape where you lay. But who could gainsay her clever ploys?

She feigns this way and that, dragging her wing tip
in a sinuous line, hopscotching across the plain.

Thinking ourselves clever, we become fox,
taste the sweet flesh of this poor, earth-bound creature.

Following, we travel ever further from satisfaction.

Even you, dumb egg, play the decoy, lying
in the gravel, silent as any stone.

Soon, little one, you will put on your twin yoke
and meet the light, singing your mother's wiles.

Northern Harrier
Circus cyaneus

White, nearly round as a cue ball, your egg might
roll true on that green tableland banked behind dykes—

Tantramar, maritime prairie the sea laid down,
grain by grain, when the tide was 'asking high.'

You tilt above this reclaimed place
like a bubble in a spirit level,

tipping by degrees, as if pondering
a question of loyalty, reparation for past injustice.

You yourself suspend the laws of nature,
hanging in the sky, stalled

on upswept wings,
calling all the shots.

Wash day

After forty-seven years
the laundry tub gave out.
Just like that.
Finally, my mother said,
like she'd been waiting for this day
to dispense her standard line:
Well, nothing lasts forever.
Just think of all the uses
for that phrase—infatuations,
lilacs, good ice for skating—
the curiously strong lozenge
she always had ready
to clear our minds of grief.
(Cool as peppermint, she was,
the day I left my husband.)
But I'd have to say
that in the family inventory
of things that didn't last,
the double concrete laundry tub
was the most surprising.
It sprang a leak and we said
It was bound to happen eventually
as if we really had believed
that such a simple thing could fail.
Those modern detergents, my father said,
were eating out the wire mesh
all this time.

The sound was quite a shocker,
though: metal on stone,
rising from the basement
while they whacked the thing
into pieces.
Clang
                    forty-seven years
          clang.
Tough as the dickens,
my father said, resting
the sledgehammer on the floor.
When my mother took it from his hands
he showed her where to land the blows.

The New House

You didn't like my new house. Because I packed
your childhood into two plastic bins when I moved
and even though I followed you to your new city, I left
the old house behind, the one where we both grew up.
I packed the photo albums and your kindergarten
finger paintings, your baby clothes. I packed
the videotape of your third birthday and my fortieth.
You didn't know I was afraid to pack
everything that had been pushed to the back
of the closet—or did you? You always knew
everything, knew it often before I did, the way
tears came into your eyes but didn't fall when
your father and I sang *Ode to Joy* beside your bed,
and I thought everything was okay, I said
Everything's okay, didn't I? How could I unpack
those days, remember the family you drew
for yourself before things broke—
your happy self and happy wife and happy baby.
And now here you are in the middle of your own
life, your own house—the wise life you're
constructing for yourself, for someone you love,
someone who loves you back, with work,
and friends, and food. I like my new house,
even though you're not in it very often.
I want your new life, all the good things
you've put in it. Maybe I have one too.
What can we do with the old life
but make ourselves a better one?

Leitmotiv

Tonight we watched a halfway-decent movie
concerning loss of memory and/or love
driving our sheathed nerve-endings to approve
an ending we didn't quite loathe or believe.
There was a gait to the movie, a groove
that slit our wits by shortwave
slotting our thoughts through its intricate sieve.
We were enthralled and galled, at one remove.

Between barren groves of firm resolve
and a liberal vale of stoic reserve
we'd been moved. We met at the stove
for cheese-toast and tea. All critiques saved
by the window's moon-blaze: It was grand, grave,
and granted our silence something substantive.

One and One

For every one there is a one, and one
and one make one, divided.

For every one a one must die, and every
death is one, provided

every other is a one and one
is every other.

An other and a one make one,
husbanded and brided.

The union of a one and one
makes other, suicided.

Self-murder of the one-in-one is mother
of the other one and one

another's one-in-ones conspire to smother
other ones, while lovers

wire their one and ones
implacably together.

One is bound and gagged by one, one
saws and frays the knot

of one, and one
lets slip the tether.

after George Herbert

Missed connections: Walmart automotive dept—w4m

You. At the Tire and Lube Express. You said *lube*
and I—did you notice?—revved. Your name tag
was missing so I read your hair, curled like a string of *e*'s,
your forearms drizzled with soft hairs like a boy's
first moustache. Apart from that, you were built
like a walrus. The kind of man that drives a Ford
pickup. Black or silver. You said, *There might be a gas leak*
and *We can't fix that here, but don't worry, we'll get you fixed.*
By *fixed* you meant *hooked up,* by *hooked up* you meant
in touch with and meant nothing beyond *touch.*

Me. Volvo. Smelled like gasoline: I overfilled the tank
before the oil change. I took the package that comes
with a filter replacement. Have you already forgotten me?
I had trouble with the debit machine. Remember? You said,
Turn your card the other way—remember?—and took my hand,
not the card, took my hand with the card in it
and swiped it through. Remember. Please.
The gasoline. The woman almost on fire.

A Crow's Life

No romantic, he warned me right off—
Cuckoo, hitch your wagon to this star,

and it's a crow's life, all dirty tricks
and rot-gut cuisine, snaffling up

the last slice of pepperoni pizza. Now
I'm stuck here, tree-high, nest-bound,

bored out of my violet-flecked head, but, hey,
someone's got to do it, sit on these eggs.

Plunderers everywhere. Turn your back
and a blue jay will rob you blind. I don't believe

in happiness but I do caw something
like joy when I see his glossiness pummeling

the dusk-sharp distance, I do weep
glad tears when he's winging toward me,

banana or road kill clamped between his beak.
Love him or leave him? You tell me.

His cornfields and back alley dumpsters,
his thieving genius and high wire acts,

the showy, pyrotechnic stunts.
This life with this crow—

witty as a pickpocket, shiny as tin foil.
Oh my dark carrion, circling, circling.

Awaiting

There is a long wait of the passengers
For the detouring and delayed bus
And the wait of the wintry grasses

The wait of the legendary lion king
Before it preys upon a real baby zebra
And the wait of the summer sun deep in the nightmare

The wait of the orchid on the window ledge
The wait of the diamond in an unknown mine
And the wait where you stop and watch

And there is a wait of this darkness
Which you are going to compress into words
A wait that is to spread out thin on the blank paper

Unlike winter stars holding their light in light-years
The wait after you finish writing
And the longer wait then

Notes & Bios

BALL, JONATHAN

"Salvador Dali Lama"

One of those poems that result from Freudian slips in conversation, a joke you don't realize you've made until it's on the table beside your whiskey. Although Christian Bök (who, if I remember correctly, I was talking to when this title slipped out) likes to disparage Dali as a van artist, I suspect he's just mad that Dali beat him to the title *Diary of a Genius*. On a personal level, as a child from a small and isolated town in Northwestern Ontario, Dali was my gateway drug to the avant-garde.

Bio:

Jonathan Ball, Ph.D., is the author of *Ex Machina* (BookThug, 2009), *Clockfire* (Coach House Books, 2010), and *The Politics of Knives* (Coach House Books, 2012). Visit him online at www.jonathanball.com or @jonathanballcom.

BESNER, LINDA

"Wartime Puppet Play"

I was interested in the moral quandary of depicting war, and in how (especially with the Second World War) a sort of warm nostalgia can set in that miniaturizes and domesticates the reality. Somehow it seems to get mixed up with British grandparents and tea cosies and starts to seem like a design element in a period stage set. I wanted to take this idea to an extreme and present violent conflict in a way that gave it an almost claymation feel. I tried to use brand names or emblematic colour schemes that would allow kitchen items to stand in for nationalities—I was thinking of Guantanamo with the Arabic-speaking black-and-white checked dishrag (meant to evoke the keffiyeh, a traditional scarf in many Middle Eastern countries). I was also thinking about how the "folksy" traditions we're nostalgic for bleed so easily into ein volk, the nationalistic idea of "one people" that underpinned the Nazi movement. That quaint, casual kitchen-table racism has re-emerged in the last decade or so as kitsch; Urban Outfitters frequently makes headline news by putting out "joke" t-shirts with retro-racist slogans. In constructing the poem, my intention was to give the first stanza the energy and humour of a puppet show as children's entertainment. I hoped for the second stanza to undercut this effect by showing the destruction left by the events in the first stanza, and to remind us of the ugly attitudes of the era by bringing in the line of racist epithets. Contemporary puppet shows for adults can be dark and frightening, and part of their power is the uncanny quality of physical objects invested with human speech and emotions. I tried to borrow some of that uncanniness here.

Bio:

Linda Besner is originally from Wakefield, Quebec. Her poetry and reviews have appeared in *The Walrus, Maisonneuve,* and *The Malahat Review* among other journals. Her radio work has aired on CBC's Definitely Not the Opera, Outfront, and The Next Chapter. Her first collection of poetry, *The Id Kid,* was published in 2011 by Véhicule Press, and was named as one of The National Post's Best Poetry Books of the Year. She lives in Toronto.

BOLSTER, STEPHANIE

"Gardening"

I'd rather write poems about gardens than do the work a garden requires, a preference I was forced to confront after moving to a suburb. Add an infestation of white grubs, a lifelong

Notes & Bios

squeamishness about squirmy things, and a writing project that required me to interrogate my equally lifelong fascination with the intersection of the made and the natural, and I ended up with what would become this poem. I made up the foxgloves, though I can no longer remember why I believed the poem needed them. (Something, perhaps, about the fact that they are ubiquitous intruders in my parents' garden, that they are both beautiful and poisonous, and that the word in itself offers a Beatrix Potter-esque suggestion of that intersection of the made and the natural.) I've also forgotten how many drafts this poem went through, though I know there were more than enough to reaffirm my admiration for Pound's winnowing down of "In a Station of the Metro." I know, too, that without Alison Strumberger having solicited my work for the "Wild" issue of Branch (thank you, Alison!), this little poem would have remained in the darkness of my hard drive for a long time, if not forever.

Bio:

Stephanie Bolster's most recent book, *A Page from the Wonders of Life on Earth*, was shortlisted for the Pat Lowther Award in 2012. Her first book, *White Stone: The Alice Poems*, won the Governor General's Award and the Gerald Lampert Award in 1998. The recipient of the Bronwen Wallace and Archibald Lampman Awards and The Malahat Review's long poem prize, among others, her work been translated into French, Spanish, and German. She edited *The Best Canadian Poetry in English 2008*—the inaugural anthology in this series—as well as *The Ishtar Gate: Last and Selected Poems* by the Ottawa poet Diana Brebner, and co-edited *Penned: Zoo Poems*. Raised in Burnaby, B.C., she teaches creative writing at Concordia University and lives in Pointe-Claire, Québec.

BOXER, ASA

"The Beach is a Rake"

"The Beach is a Rake" was originally published in *Skullduggery*—a word meaning "dirty dealing." It is a short love poem with humourous undertones appearing in a series of such pieces that use the ocean as a vehicle to probe the depth and chaos of feeling.

Bio:

Asa Boxer's poetry has garnered several prizes and has been included in various anthologies, including *The Best Canadian Poetry in English, 2009*. His books are *The Mechanical Bird* (Signal Editions, 2007), and, most recently, *Skullduggery* (Signal, 2011).

COOK, GEOFFREY

"The Breakup of the Ice"

"You cannot step into the same river twice"—Heraclitus

I am writing this in Tidnish Bridge at my uncle's house where my poem is set. Only the river seems not to have changed: my father is now 70; the children are young adults; I am almost 50, and, though married, childless, as the poem foresaw. I have always felt my poems are "ahead of me," that my life needed to catch up to whatever wisdom my poetry revealed. For in its madeness (and reading is a making), in its aesthetic coherence, a poem implies a fatedness and consummation that exposes life's contingency and unfinishedness, its flailing about for meaningful destiny.

The poem was written backwards from the final stanza— a recognition of love's potential to heal and redeem and of its apparent failure to actually do anything (making love analogous to poetry). I thought I was writing a sonnet, but realized the climactic quatrain required more context to achieve the right emotional effect. So I found myself writing a narrative poem and nearly "naming names," something I avoided in the past. Alden Nowlan wrote in "And He Wept Aloud So That the Egyptians Heard It," "Oh, admit this man, there's no point in poetry / if you withhold the truth / once you've come by it." Poetry is a way of "coming by" the truth; in admitting it, poetry achieves its moral purpose. A poem becomes "true" not through transcribing the literal, but in discovering how to speak truth. I rarely know what I want to say in writing a poem, just that an image or a rhythm wants to be said; and only in language taking form have I learned what I'm saying and tried to say it 'true'.

This makes poetry analogous to life: we learn belatedly. Whether the result will forgive us for "learning we've not loved enough," and we will be embraced—in dreams, in the Underworld—I don't know.

Bio

Geoffrey Cook's poetry has most recently appeared in *Fiddlehead* # 247, Spring 2011, and in the anthology *Approaches to Poetry: the pre-poem moment* (Frog Hollow Press: 2009). His translations of German poetry have appeared in Exile Quarterly Vol. 35, # 2 (2011), The Antigonish Review #166, Summer 2011, and the anthology *The Exile Book of Poems in Translation* (Exile: 2009). Geoff's book of poetry, *Postscript* (Véhicule/Signal: 2004), was nominated for national awards and widely anthologized. "The Break Up of the Ice on the Tidnish River" was shortlisted for the 2009 Winston Collins/ Descant Prize for Best Canadian Poem. Raised in Nova Scotia, Geoff lives in the Laurentians and teaches English.

COUTURE, DANI

"Salvage"

Bio:

Dani Couture is the author of two collections of poetry: *Good Meat* (Pedlar Press, 2006) and *Sweet* (Pedlar Press, 2010). *Sweet* was named one of Maisy's Best Books of 2010 by *Maisonneuve Magazine* and nominated for the Trillium Book Award for Poetry; *Sweet* won the ReLit Award for poetry. In 2011, Dani also received an Honour of Distinction from The Writers' Trust Dayne Ogilvie Grant. Her debut novel, *Algoma*, was published in fall 2011 by Invisible Publishing. Couture is the Literary Editor of *THIS Magazine*.

DICKINSON, ADAM

"Call to Arms"

"Call to Arms" is from my forthcoming book *The Polymers* (Anansi, 2013), which is structured as an imaginary science project that examines the intersection between chemicals and poetry, specifically plastics. The poems express the repeating structures fundamental to plastic molecules as they appear in cultural and linguistic behaviours such as arguments, anxieties, and trends. "Call to Arms" is an anxious response to an accident victim's prosthetic limbs. Its repetitions and obsessions constitute a polymeric form.

Bio:

Adam Dickinson is a writer, researcher and teacher. His poems have appeared in literary journals in Canada and internationally as well as in anthologies such as *Breathing Fire 2: Canada's New Poets* and *The Shape of Content: Creative Writing in Mathematics and Science*. His

Notes & Bios

collection *Kingdom, Phylum* was a finalist for the Trillium Book Award for Poetry. His next book, *The Polymers*, will be published in the spring of 2013. He is also working on another poetry project that involves testing his blood and body for chemicals and microbes. When not giving his body to science, he teaches at Brock University in St. Catharines, Ontario.

DODDS, JERAMY

"The Swan with Two Necks"

"The Swan with Two Necks" is a true account of an event, in which I participated, that occurred at Tjörnin (The Pond) in Reykjavík, Iceland, during August 12th of 2010. Due to a prohibitive "gag clause," and subsequent witness disappearances believed to be executed through the co-operative efforts of SHIELD and SAG-AFTRA, I recount this event at great possible peril to both Mr. Walken and myself.

Bio:

Jeramy Dodds is the author of *Crabwise to the Hounds* (Coach House Books, 2008).

ELLISON, JOANNE

"True Confessions"

Not usually a fan of rhymed poetry, I've always loved the villanelle, especially since Elizabeth Bishop added humor and lightness to the form. This villanelle was written on the proverbial scrap of paper while I was sitting with my husband in the Golden Tulip Hotel in Ghana, West Africa. It was a clingingly hot day and the service in the restaurant was witheringly slow, so it was pleasant to imagine escaping to cooler, more northerly climates. Of course, escape leads always back to new boundaries...or so the poem professes.

Bio:

Joanne Ellison is a poet and teacher who lives in Edmonton with her easy-going husband, who doesn't mind being praised or castigated in her poetry, and a very attractive cat, who continually meows complaints about her share of royalties. Joanne has previously published her work with *Rubicon Press*, *Leaf Press*, *Nashwaak Review*, and *CV2*. She has great respect for editors and publishers who work so selflessly to showcase Canadian poetry.

FORMAN, GABE

"Dish Bitches"

This poem started from a few lines featuring sets of culinary words and phrases like 'apricots', 'foaming pots' and 'countertops'. As I wrote them, I was mostly horsing around with the sounds of these kitchen words without trying to say anything overly specific about being a human dishwasher, a position which I have held on several occasions since I was in my teens. I have often felt that the work of the dishwasher was monotonous, but its repetitions could also be meditative, even satisfying. Standing in front of a heap of dirty plates or glasses or pans was often a good environment for daydreaming and imagination. As "Dish Bitches" took shape, this more cerebral aspect of the dishwasher's job started to creep into the some of the lines. Eventually, the contrast between the grittiness of the sink and the highfalutin fantasies of the life of the mind became something of a theme in the poem's construction.

Notes & Bios

Bio :

Gabe Foreman grew up in Thunder Bay. His collection, *A Complete Encyclopedia of Different Types of People* (Coach House Books) was awarded the 2011 A.M. Klein Prize for Poetry and was a finalist for the Concordia University First Book Prize. He lives in Montreal.

GILLIS, SUSAN
"Solstice Night"

To me, the solstices always feel sort of apocalyptic: edgy, anything-can-happen-ish. This is one of the first poems to come out of my experience living in rural Ontario, where winter and night have their own language. I hadn't imagined falling in love with winter when I moved to central Canada from the BC coast, but I did, first in Montreal (whose metro concourses form one of the stages of this poem) and now in the farm country of Lanark County. The winter solstice is an important (and paradoxical) time—light begins to grow while the hardest weather is yet to come.

Bio:

Susan Gillis is a poet, teacher, and member of the poetry collective *Yoko's Dogs*. *Volta* (Signature, 2002) won the A. M. Klein Prize for Poetry. Her most recent books are *The Rapids* (Brick, 2012) and *Twenty Views of the Lachine Rapids* (Gaspereau, 2012). *Whisk*, in collaboration with *Yoko's Dogs*, is forthcoming from Pedlar Press in 2013. Susan divides her time between Montreal and a hamlet near Perth, Ontario.

"Solstice Night" will be published in *The Rapids*, by Brick Books, September 2012.

GRAHAM, LAURIE D
"Say Here, Here"

This bruiser jumped into the boat while I was working on an MFA in writing with the University of Guelph and living in a cheap apartment surrounded by mansions in the Forest Hill Village neighbourhood of Toronto. I had for about a week a perilously unsaved Word document open on my laptop at the kitchen table/my office, and every time I got near it I'd add another line, a few more words, another image. It was writing by accretion (which was unusual for me), big and enraged (not as unusual). I did a fair bit of pacing. Tough because the apartment was very small. That was step one.

I can't recall the point at which I noticed this poem was trying to talk about property, possession, land—specifically prairie land and loss—but from early on the poem strained to be chronological (albeit with massive, unaccountable gaps) and fast like time-lapse photography. The repetition of the imperative *say*, by no means an original device (see Lisa Robertson's *The Weather* for a much better example), might provide an anchor through all the jumps between images, or lend rhythm or tension through repetition, or entreat the reader to form the words, to row into that place herself. Those *say*s refuse to sit nicely though, and the lines reject the smooth break, in spite of my numerous attempts to tidy them up. This poem wants nothing to do with tidy.

Notes & Bios

Bio:

Laurie D Graham grew up in Sherwood Park, Alberta, and now lives in Toronto, where she writes, reviews, edits, and teaches. Her first book of poetry, *Field,* will be out with Hagios Press in 2013. She's currently at work on a new series of poems about the Northwest Resistance.

GREENE, RICHARD
"Corrections"

The poem "Corrections" is based on current conditions and recent events in a federal prison in Canada.

Bio:

Richard Greene was born in Newfoundland and lives now in Cobourg, Ontario. His third collection of poetry *Boxing the Compass* (Signal Editions) won the 2010 Governor General's Literary Award for Poetry. That book contained the long poem "Over the Border" which describes his journeys through the United States by Greyhound and Amtrak in the period following 9-11. Greene's biography of the poet Edith Sitwell has recently been published to international acclaim.

HENDERSON, MATHEW
"The Tank"

"The Tank" is a poem about production testing in the Alberta/Saskatchewan oilfield.

Bio:

Mathew Henderson is a recent grad of the University of Guelph's MFA program. Originally from Prince Edward Island, he now lives in Toronto, writes about the prairies and teaches at Humber College. His first collection of poetry, *The Lease,* is forthcoming from Coach House Books in the Fall of 2012.

HICKEY, DAVID
"X-Ray"

I like the idea that my body is some kind of wetsuit I've been wearing around my whole life. It makes me think I could probably float pretty far if I had to, and that if I ever take up surfing— hey, it could happen!—I'd already be well ahead of the game. That's mostly just wishful thinking, of course, but what better way to make a living.

Bio:

David Hickey is the author of two poetry collections, *In the Lights of a Midnight Plow* (2006) and *Open Air Bindery* (2011). Originally from Prince Edward Island, he now lives in London, Ontario.

JERNIGAN, AMANDA
"Aubade"

I first circulated "Aubade" in a limited-edition letterpress pamphlet, alongside a photograph by my husband, John Haney. The photograph shows a threshold between water and land; the scale is indeterminate: we could be looking at an aerial photograph of a coastline, or at a close-up of a tidal pool. "Aubade" subsequently became the first poem in the sequence "First Principals," set in and out of an unorthodox Garden of Eden. The sequence appears in full in my book *Groundwork: poems*.

Bio:

Amanda Jernigan is the author of *Groundwork: poems* (Biblioasis, 2011), and of a new book of poems forthcoming from Cormorant. She lives in Hamilton, Ontario.

JOHNSTONE, JIM
"Inland"

Frederick Banting, the co-discoverer of insulin, died of exposure following a plane crash in 1941. Inland reimagines the aftermath of the accident.

Bio:

Jim Johnstone is a Toronto-based writer and physiologist. He's the author of three books of poetry: *Sunday, the locusts* (Tightrope Books, 2011), *Patternicity* (Nightwood Editions, 2010) and *The Velocity of Escape* (Guernica Editions, 2008) and the winner of several national awards including a CBC Literary Award and *The Fiddlehead*'s Ralph Gustafson Poetry Prize. From 2005 to 2011 he curated *Misunderstandings Magazine*, a lit zine he co-founded with Ian Williams and Vicki Sloot. Currently, he's the Poetry Editor at Palimpsest Press.

KOTSILIDIS, LEIGH
"By Any Name"

This poem emerged from research about the Cecropia moth and the discovery that even as adults they will never develop a mouth. Their only purpose is to reproduce and, in most cases, with the first of their species they encounter. Other than their sex, there is nothing special which makes one Cecropia moth stand apart from another. I thought this was an apt metaphor for human behaviour (in a tongue-in-cheek way, of course), with the exception that as humans we tend to think we are more sophisticated than perhaps we actually are.

Bio:

Leigh Kotsilidis grew up in Niagara Falls, Ontario. Her poems have appeared in several literary journals and Canadian anthologies. In 2009 and 2010 she was selected as a finalist for the CBC Literary Awards. She is also co-founder of littlefishcartpress. *Hypotheticals,* her first full length poetry collection, was published by Coach House books in the Fall of 2011. She currently lives in Montreal where she works as a freelance graphic designer.

LAHEY, ANITA
"Care Package"

Before my husband (we were not yet married) left for his 2010 tour in Afghanistan as a combat engineer with the Canadian military, we visited the Redpath Museum on McGill's campus in downtown Montreal several times, charmed and fascinated by its elegant domed interior, its meticulous and informative displays, and the range of its collection through geology, anthropology, natural history: its flavour of having once belonged to a learned Victorian gentleman with eclectic interests. I continued to visit the museum while "Capt Good" was away, and while I became more and more frustrated with not just the war itself but with the assumptions and presumptions people make about soldiers and global conflicts and the "loved ones" left behind. These two phenomena, mixed, I'm sure, with my own fraught emotions, blended into this utterly impractical poetic "care package": all the things—not toothpaste, not foot powder or kits for "movie night at the FOB" or iPod earbuds (as one well-meaning blogger advised)—that I would send him, this one soldier among thousands, were it in my power. There was more impulse than design at work, and I suspect what this (lengthy! emphatic! hear me out!) poem sequence is trying to say, not just to my husband but to all warriors and those who sign their orders, is not any different from what has been urged upon them for centuries: here are the things that matter, and that we hope will continue to matter. Drop your weapons and come home.

Bio:

Anita Lahey's second collection of poems, *Spinning Side Kick*, was released by Véhicule Press in 2011. Her first book, *Out to Dry in Cape Breton* (2006), was nominated for the Trillium Book Award for Poetry and the Ottawa Book Award, and she is a past winner of the Great Blue Heron Poetry Prize and the Ralph Gustafson Prize for Best Poem. She served as editor of Arc Poetry Magazine from 2004 to 2011, and is also a journalist who has written on a wide range of topics for publications such as *The Walrus*, *Cottage Life*, *Maisonneuve*, *Toronto Life*, *Reader's Digest*, *Canadian Geographic* and *Quill & Quire*. A former resident of Ottawa, Montreal and Fredericton, she lives in Toronto.

LEBOWITZ, RACHEL

from Cottonopolis: "Tablecloth, Jar, Cask, Muslin Dress, Photograph,Negro"

These poems are from a book sequence of prose-and-found poems about the Industrial Revolution, specifically the links between the cotton industry in Lancashire and slavery. I've combed many history books for arresting images: vultures resting on rusted guns at the British slave fort Cape Coast Castle, slaves' bodies shining with palm oil (to make them appear healthier than they were so they could be sold), dying slave ship sailors huddled in sugar casks, buyers moving slaves' fingers back and forth to see how well they'll pick cotton—these are poems already! I bring them here, add new details, toss in some harsh words here, some hibicus there. The art of it is important to me but mostly it is my hope that through this, the stories will still be heard.

Bio:

Rachel Lebowitz is the author of *Hannus* (Pedlar Press, 2006) which was shortlisted for the 2007 Roderick Haig-Brown Regional Prize (BC Book Prize) and the Edna Staebler Award for Creative Non-Fiction. She is also the co-author, with Zachariah Wells, of the children's picture book *Anything But Hank!* (Biblioasis, 2008, illustrated by Eric Orchard). The poems published here come from her upcoming book, *Cottonopolis* (Pedlar Press, Spring 2013). She lives in Halifax.

LISTA, MICHAEL

"The Scarborough Bluffs"

"The Scarborough Bluffs" is from a collection of poems set in the Greater Toronto Area on Easter weekend 1992.

Bio:

Michael Lista is the author of *Bloom*, published by the House of Anansi. Poems from his forthcoming book, *The Scarborough Bluffs*, are appearing in *Poetry* magazine. He lives in Toronto, where he is the poetry editor of *The Walrus*, and the poetry columnist at *The National Post*.

LITHGOW, MICHAEL ANDREW

"Cradle and light"

I wrote this poem shortly after my father had a stroke a few years ago. I was on my way to visit him, on the train from Montreal to Ottawa, a beautiful rural countryside. There was something about moving towards loss … It was my first real encounter with the possibility of the death of one of my parents, an inkling of the enormous absence and loss that comes with that event and that nothing really prepares us for … Watching and listening to the children playing in the dying light coupled with my flickering sense of dread, the still beauty of the landscape, and the movement of the train, invoked in me a sense of the cycles of life, of joy and loss unfolding endlessly from the motions of our lives.

Bio:

Michael Andrew Lithgow's poetry has appeared in *Arc Magazine, The New Quarterly, Fiddlehead* and *CV2*. Selections of his work have been included in *Undercurrents: New Voices in Canadian Poetry* (Cormorant Books, 2010), and *Rutting Season* (Buffalo Runs Press, 2009). His first solo collection, *Waking in the Tree House,* was published in Spring 2012 by Cormorant Books. He is a contributing editor at ArtThreat.net and a research associate with the Canadian Alternative Media Archive. Michael is a PhD candidate in the School of Journalism and Communication studying aesthetics and dissent in digital and performance cultures.

LUSH, LAURA

"Small Story"

I have always enjoyed writing short "haiku-like" poems that can pack in a lot of meaning in a short space. For "Small Story," I wanted to show how a tree can reflect the natural rhythms of life.

Bio:

Laura Lush lives in Guelph and teaches Academic English and Creative Writing at the University of Toronto's School of Continuing Studies. "Small Story" is from her fourth collection of poems entitled *Carapace,* published by Palimpsest Press in 2011.

MARCHARD, KIRYA

"Hamlet"

This poem represents an exploration of its own textuality. Silly, self-reflexive, and fun to say out loud, "Hamlet" is a response to a question posed by James McLaverty and put forward again by Jerome McGann in his work, *The Textual Condition: "If the Mona Lisa is hanging in the Louvre in Paris, where is Hamlet?"* The reader is hence invited to follow a trail of clues that leads from Shakespeare's studio all the way to the pocketbooks of modern day Beijing, all in

Notes & Bios

pursuit of the melancholic prince. By the end, the reader should be more aware of both Hamlet's odd elusiveness and ubiquity, and of the role we ourselves play in his ongoing history.

Bio:

Kirya Marchand is a 22 year-old poet born and raised in Montreal. She is currently pursuing her Bachelor's degree at McGill University, double-majoring in English Literature and Environmental Sciences. A part-time educator, environmental activist, and poet of nature, her work has previously appeared in *Room Magazine, The Antigonish Review, GRAIN, Poetry Quebec*, and on CBC Radio.

MATUK, NYLA
"Don Draper"

"Don Draper" was inspired by the protagonist of the stylized and provocative American television drama Mad Men.

Bio:

Nyla Matuk was born in Winnipeg in 1967 and educated at McGill University, where she earned an M.A. in English and won the Lionel Shapiro Prize for short fiction. She has worked as a magazine editor, freelance writer, and college English instructor, and in corporate communications, refugee claims, and public policy. Her writing has appeared in *ARC Poetry, The Walrus, Maisonneuve, Prism International, Descant*, the *Globe and Mail*, and elsewhere. A chapbook, *Oneiric*, was published in 2009 by Frog Hollow Press. *Sumptuary Laws* (Véhicule Press, 2012) is her first full-length collection of poetry.

MCCARTNEY, SHARON
"Katahdin"

"Katahdin" was written in the aftermath of a relationship that didn't work. A perfectly nice guy, perfectly respectable and desirable, but it just didn't work and that was distressing for me. Whatever distresses me ends up in a poem. Mt. Katahdin is Maine's highest mountain and the northern terminus of the Appalachian Trail. It's a big mountain (5,268 feet or 1,606 metres). Climbing it took about nine hours, I think. But we (the perfectly nice guy and I) started from New Brunswick at 3 a.m. so a long day. I liked the metaphor of the mountain, because he was a guy who was happy to be at the top, to relax and enjoy the view. And I couldn't. I wanted to get on with the task ahead. Which was getting back down and on with my life. I trust that he's happier without me.

Bio:

Sharon McCartney is the author of *For and Against* (2010, Goose Lane Editions), *The Love Song of Laura Ingalls Wilder* (2007, Nightwood Editions), *Karenin Sings the Blues* (2003, Goose Lane Editions) and *Under the Abdominal Wall* (1999, Anvil Press). A new collection of poetry is forthcoming from Palimpsest Press in Spring 2013. In 2008, she received the Acorn/Plantos People's Prize for poetry for *The Love Song of Laura Ingalls Wilder*. She lives in Fredericton, New Brunswick.

MCGIMPSEY, DAVID

"What Was That Poem"

My mother, Mary Macdonald McGimpsey, knew the lines to many, many poems and songs. She attended Montreal High School in the 1930s and reciting poems was a core part of her—as she would amusingly say—"Victorian education." She lived with the great spirit of the working class who sought education not just to fit one's self into a career but to better one's self by enjoying the good things in life. She was as comfortable listening to the opera as she was listening to a ballgame. My poem tries to commemorate her spirit and tries to do so with manners I am certain she was proud of.

Bio:

David McGimpsey lives in Montreal and is the author of five collections of poetry including *Li'l Bastard* (Coach House Books) which was named as one of the "books of the year" by both *The Quill and Quire* and *The National Post*. David has a PhD in English Literature and is the author of the award-winning study *Imagining Baseball: America's Pastime and Popular Culture*. David writes a regular humor column called "The Self-Esteem Workout" for Matrix and is contributing editor for *EnRoute* magazine, where he writes about sandwiches and travel. In addition to being the author of one collection of short fiction (*Certifiable*), David is the Montreal fiction editor of the e-magazine *Joyland* and is the fiction editor for the Punchy Writers Series of DC Books. David was named by the CBC as one of the "Top Ten English language poets in Canada" and his work was also the subject of the recent book of essays *Population Me: Essays on David McGimpsey* (Palimpsest Press). David teaches creative writing and literature at Concordia University.

MOONEY, JACOB MCARTHUR

"Unisphere at Midnight"

Every ten years or so, someone tries to climb the Unisphere in Queens, NY. Sometimes they survive, but other times they don't. This guy didn't. I've always had a thing for Worlds Fairs.

Bio:

Jacob McArthur Mooney's books are *The New Layman's Almanac* (McClelland & Stewart, 2008) and *Folk* (M&S, 2011), the latter of which was a finalist for the Dylan Thomas Prize and the Trillium Book Award in Poetry.

MURRAY, GEORGE

"Belfast"

"Belfast" is part of an ongoing series of poems named after cities I have lived in or have a deep relationship with. Others include "Toronto", "St. John's", "New York", etc. The poems mentally reconstruct each city in a pastiche fashion by riddling my atmospheric impressions with literal, but often incongruous, observations, anecdotes, images, etc. In the end, I hope to provide a "sense" of Belfast, rather than its story.

Bio:

George Murray is the author of six books of poetry, most recently: *Whiteout* (ECW, 2012), *Glimpse: Selected Aphorisms* (ECW, 2010), *The Rush to Here* (Nightwood, 2007), and *The*

Notes & Bios

Hunter (McClelland & Stewart, 2003). His work appears widely in journals and anthologies in Canada, the US, the UK, Europe, and the Antipodes. He lives in St. John's, Newfoundland.

O'MEARA, DAVID

"Background Noise"

Whether it's war or neurosis, one has to engage with something in order to defeat it. But any deep engagement reveals complexity. This poem originates in superficial irritation and dilates obsessively toward discoveries of "cosmic microwave background radiation," evidence of the Big Bang. I have loosely referenced the "Holmdel Horn Antenna" (look it up on Wikipedia; it's pretty cool) and the experiments done at Bell Labs in the 1950s.

Bio:

David O'Meara is the author of three poetry collections, most recently *Noble Gas, Penny Black* with Brick Books (2008). A new collection is due in fall 2013 with Coach House Books. He lives in Ottawa.

ORMSBY, ERIC

"Some Birds"

"Some Birds" is part of a collection of poems on our feathered friends, now in progress, with the working title *A Commonwealth of Wing*.

Bio:

Eric Ormsby is the author of seven collections of poems, most recently *The Baboons of Hada* (Carcanet, 2011). He has also published two collections of essays: *Facsimiles of Time: Essays on Poetry and Translation* (2001) and *Fine Incisions: Essays on Poetry and Place* (2011), both published by The Porcupine's Quill. His translation of the last work of the eleventh-century Persian poet and philosopher Nasir Khosraw has just appeared under the title *Between Reason and Revelation:Twin Wisdoms Reconciled* (I.B. Tauris, 2012). A longtime resident of Montreal, he now lives in London.

PARTRIDGE, ELISE

"Range"

This poem is about a kind and generous appliance repairman whose skill, passion, and ingenuity rescued a 1940s range in Vancouver.

Bio:

Elise Partridge is the author of *Fielder's Choice* (Signal; shortlisted for the Lampert Award) and *Chameleon Hours* (Anansi; nominated for the Livesay Poetry Prize and winner of the Canadian Authors Association Poetry Award). Her work has been anthologized in *The Best Canadian Poetry in English 2009* and elsewhere in Canada, the US, the UK, and Ireland. Recently she was Poet-in-Residence for *Arc Magazine*.

PURDHAM, MEDRIE

"Bear Room"

My poem "Bear Room," which depicts my grandfather's taxidermied specimens, was written out of my interest in poetry as a vehicle for the expression of ambivalent experience.

Bio:

Medrie Purdham teaches at the University of Regina. Her poetry has been published in *The New Quarterly*, *The Malahat Review*, *The Fiddlehead*, *Grain*, *The Antigonish Review* and in other Canadian literary journals. She sews costumes and is interested in miniatures.

RHODES, SHANE

"Paperweight"

I still remember this trip to Winnipeg clearly: it was after spring seeding, my parents had driven 16 hours the day before to get there, and my father took us to the Winnipeg Grain Exchange to see the prices of wheat, barley, oats and rape seed blink on the overhead flicker board. I think it was a trip my father had wanted to make all his life, to finally see his work (full of doubt, worry, dirt, dust and grease) transcend to the cleanliness of numbers. As we watched, the commodity traders on the other side of the viewing glass looked up from their numbers in boredom and smiled. Later that day, I bought this paperweight. It is on my desk even now. I still don't know what to do with it.

Bio:

Shane Rhodes is the author, most recently, of *Err.* Shane's poetry has won an Alberta Book Award, two Lampman Awards, the P. K. Page Founder's Award for Poetry, and a National Magazine Gold Award. He is the poetry editor for *Arc*, Canada's national poetry magazine.

ROBERTSON, LISA

"Scene"

"Scene" describes a late spring in the Vienne region of France, my home. Its dedicatee, Ted Byrne, had asked me to describe the scene of writing. I thought of the equivocation that surrounded me, economically, naturally and socially, and this was my delayed response.

Bio:

Lisa Robertson lives in France. Her books of poetry include *Debbie: An Epic,* which was a finalist for the Governor General's Award for Poetry, *The Weather*, winner of the Relit Award, *Lisa Robertson's Magenta Soul Whip*, one of the New York Times 100 best books of 2010, and *R's Boat.* She has published two books of essays, *Occasional Works* and *Seven Walks from the Office for Soft Architecture, and Nilling.* She is also a writer and collaborator in the visual and media arts.

RUTHIG, INGRID

"Academic Liaison"

Poets have magpie-like habits, gathering moments, ideas, images, emotions, sounds, words. It's sometimes hard to tell which glittering curiosity, which shiny bit of ephemera will spark a new piece of writing. Several years and versions later, it's even harder to recall what prompted "Academic Liaison". Sifting through my notebooks reveals no clues; just the original title, "Triangulation", and a few initial lines. Maybe a story or detail long since reabsorbed into the Cloud set things rolling; I can't say for sure. I do know that I'm fascinated by that instant in which people connect or make a decision, and the why of it all is often easier to explore and reveal through metaphor. During the writing and rewriting, the subconscious takes over, to some degree, and that's when the good stuff happens. This piece examines points of recognition,

Notes & Bios

as when someone sees a chance to reclaim sense of self or direction. I'll leave it at that, so the reader can make his/her own connection.

Bio:

Ingrid Ruthig's work has been widely published, won a Petra Kenney International Poetry Prize, and includes the poem sequence and artist's book *Slipstream* (Arkitexwerks, 2011), *Richard Outram—Essays on His Works* (Guernica, 2011) and *Synesthete II* (Littlefishcart Press, 2005). A former architect and an editor of Lichen Arts & Letters Preview from 2000-2007, she currently is an associate editor for Northern Poetry Review. She lives near Toronto.

SOLIE, KAREN
"Lift Up Your Eyes"

"Lift Up Your Eyes" grew from an incident in my home town several years ago. I'm not often faithful to the actual details of specific events, but I am here. My generation, and my parents' generation, are watching a town that was thriving—albeit very small—not terribly long ago fairly surely die. And there are people going down with it, and because of it.

Bio:

Karen Solie was born in Moose Jaw and grew up in southwest Saskatchewan. Her most recent collection of poems, *Pigeon,* won the Pat Lowther Award, the Trillium Poetry Prize, and the Griffin Prize. Her work has been published across Canada, in the U.S., the U.K., and Europe, and has been translated into French, German, Korean, and Dutch. She is an associate director for the Banff Centre's Writing Studio program, and lives in Toronto with her husband, the poet David Seymour.

STERNBERG, RICARDO
"Blues"

"Blues" is what survives of a sequence of four or five poems begun years ago and centered around a slightly decadent figure called Lord Tamarind. All the poems, like "Blues" composed of 5 tercets. Years ago on a trip to Europe I was impressed by hearing Andean musicians playing their flutes in every city I visited. The contrast between those mournful tunes sounding out in a metropolitan hubbub stayed with me.

Bio

Ricardo Sternberg has published three books of poetry, *The Invention of Honey* (1990; republished 1996, 2006) and *Map of Dreams* (1996) with Véhicule Press, and *Bamboo Church* (2003; republished 2006) with McGill-Queens University Press. *Oriole Weather,* a Lyricalmyrical chapbook, was published in 2004 with illustrations by Mara Sternberg. He lives in Toronto.

STEWART, ROBERT EARL
"A Wind–Aided Fire"

"A Wind-Aided Fire" is after James Galvin's poem "The Stagnation." It was written on Oct. 1, 2010, at the Starbucks in the Chapters Bookstore at Devonshire Mall in Windsor, Ont., using a Waterman Charleston fountain pen and Private Reserve Midnight Blue ink, in a 192 pg. ruled Moleskine notebook.

Notes & Bios

Bio

Robert Earl Stewart lives with his wife and three children in Windsor, Ont., where he is the editor of a weekly newspaper. His first collection of poetry, *Something Burned Along the Southern Border* (Mansfield Press, 2009), was shortlisted for the Gerald Lampert Memorial Award. It was followed by *Campfire Radio Rhapsody* (Mansfield Press, 2011). He is currently working on a third collection of poetry, and a novel.

SWIFT, TODD

"Riding the Escalator"

This poem was written at a very difficult time in my life. My father and uncle had recently died and I had been diagnosed with male infertility, which taken together led to a very serious depression. It all came as quite a shock. At this time my mentor Al Alvarez was on hand, to talk about these travails, and confessional poetry — he had been a friend of Plath's, Berryman's and Lowell's. We talked a lot about the voice in poetry, and the need for a shaping intelligence, as well as a passion in the work. We both agreed that poems are not therapeutic per se, but they can still be satisfying if they click into place. This poem was one of those. Based on a personal experience of mine, where my Swatch kept having to be replaced in a London shopping mall, I sensed a small metaphysical conceit could be made available, and so I wrote this. It aims to locate a lyric voice, within a relaxed formal structure of the three-line stanzas—and almost using indie movie pathos and comedy (perhaps bathos)—to achieve a sense of emotionality, if not confession. The truth was, for me, that, even at my worst, there were moments of love and goodness, that made life just bearable. I wanted the poem to be light enough in tone to convey that sense of hope, but also hint at an underlying despair.

Bio:

Todd Swift has published eight full collections of poetry including *Seaway: New and Selected Poems* (Salmon, 2008) and *When All My Disappointments Came At Once* (Tightrope Books, 2012). Swift has edited or co-edited many anthologies, including *Poetry Nation, 100 Poets Against The War*, and (with Evan Jones) *Modern Canadian Poets* (Carcanet, 2010). His poems have appeared widely, in leading publications, including *Poetry* (Chicago), *Poetry London, Poetry Review, Jacket, The Guardian*, and *The Globe and Mail*. His poems have appeared in key North American anthologies, including *The New Canon, Open Field*, and *Best Canadian Poetry 2008*. He was Oxfam GB Poet-in-residence in 2004. New publications include *Lung Jazz: The Oxfam Book of Young British Poets* (Cinnamon Press, 2011), co-edited with Kim Lockwood. He is Director of the small press Eyewear Publishing Ltd. He lives in London with his wife, Sara.

TAYLOR, BRUCE

"Little Animals"

I was given a book for my fiftieth birthday, an old copy of Clifford Dobell's lovely biography of Antony van Leeuwenhoek, the 17th-century Dutch drapier who discovered microbes. Clifford Dobell was himself a microbiologist, an ambitious scientist working in the field van Leeuwenhoek had created. In his spare time, he taught himself Dutch, and translated the old microscopist's letters into English. His book is an affectionate portrait of one curious man by another, and I found it (curiously) moving. Also, it made me want to see these "animalcules" for myself, so I sent away for a microscope. It was my birthday, after all. The things I saw in it were amazing, to me, and I put some of them in the poem I was already writing about Dobell's book about an old drapier's letters to the Royal Society about the bizarre creatures that are still living in the ditch beside my road. In the two years since, my voyeuristic fascination with "little animals" has developed into an unprofitable obsession with ciliate taxonomy, and I have spent a great deal of time recording, identifying, measuring and classifying microscopic organisms. But there it is: lives get made into books, books remake lives. All of it is, in Ted Nelson's wonderful phrase—which I quote as often as I can—"deeply intertwingled."

Bio:

Bruce Taylor is a two-time winner of the A.M. Klein Award for Poetry. He has published four books of poetry: *Getting On with the Era* (1987), *Cold Rubber Feet* (1989), *Facts* (1998), and *No End in Strangeness* (2011). He lives in Wakefield, Quebec.

THORNTON, RUSSELL

"Brothers"

My parents got married when they were in grade 11—I was born a couple of months later. They proceeded to have three more kids in quick succession, and the machinery of a standard misfortune started up and ran on after that. I grew up with three younger brothers and a single mother on income assistance. I'm a big reader of biographies and autobiographies, and it's always fascinating for me to see how destinies spin forth from people's childhoods. My siblings have all become highly successful business people. Myself? I don't know. In this poem I tried to get out something of my brothers and I and our particular little history.

Bio:

Russell Thornton is the author of *House Built of Rain* and *The Human Shore* (both from Harbour Publishing) and the forthcoming *Birds, Metals, Stones and Rain*. His poems have appeared in several anthologies, among them *Open Wide a Wilderness: Canadian Nature Poems, Rocksalt: An Anthology of Contemporary BC Poetry, The Montreal International Poetry Prize 2011 Global Anthology*, and *Poets to Poets*. He lives in North Vancouver, BC.

THURSTON, HARRY

Ova Aves Project: "Northern Harrier, Killdeer, Common Loon"

These poems first appeared in *The New Quarterly*'s Quarc Issue, which explored the intersection of the sciences and literary arts, and were subsequently collected in *Ova Aves*, published by Anchorage Press, Jolicure, New Brunswick. Thaddeus Holownia's photographs of bird eggs from the Biology Department, Mount Allison University, inspired these poems. The process of being given a subject and images to work from might seem contrary to the usual independent practice of the poet but I found it catalytic, opening up a bank of imagery from literary sources, as well as tapping into my own field experiences as a birdwatcher. This project, in fact, perfectly married my dual interests in the language of poetry and the raw material of scientific inquiry.

Bio:

Harry Thurston has been a full-time writer—poet, journalist, author, editor and playwright—for the last 35 years and has published more than twenty books of poetry and non-fiction.

Notes & Bios

His "eco-autobiography," *A Place Between The Tides, A Naturalist's Reflections on the Salt Marsh*, was winner of the 2005 Sigurd Olson Nature Writing Award in the U.S. and a finalist for the inaugural British Columbia Award for Canadian Non-Fiction. Vehicule Press/ Signal Editions published *Animals of My Own Kind, New and Selected Poems* in 2009. His most recent book , *The Atlantic Coast, A Natural History* (Greystone Books/David Suzuki Foundation, 2011), brings together much of the environmental research and writing that he has done over the last four decades from his home base in Nova Scotia.

TODKILL, ANNE MARIE
"Wash day"

Many years ago I arrived at my parents' house with a load of laundry, like a university student or something—except that I was well past that stage. I was startled to discover my elderly parents in the process of clobbering the old laundry tub in the basement and lugging it piece by piece to the curbside, ready for the garbage collectors to take away. The grim satisfaction that they appeared to be taking in this procedure—well, I'd call it an eye-opener if I really thought I knew what it meant. No doubt my mother hated the old thing and was glad to see, in a new, white, vinyl laundry tub, another token of modernity installed in her home. I felt a pointless nostalgia; even now I can remember the cool, musty smell of that cavernous old tub. But what struck me most of all, with something not unlike the whump of a sledgehammer, was how the solidarity of a marriage can express itself in unexpected ways.

Bio:

Anne Marie Todkill lives, works and writes in inner-suburban Ottawa when she isn't stumbling around in the woods and swamps of North Hastings, Ontario.

TREGEBOV, RHEA
"The New House"

I am in fact now living in a newer house than the apartment I wrote the poem in. Some of the furnishings that I've brought along to my new address can best be classified as "hand-me-ups," a term that I've heard used to describe possessions inherited from the next, rather than the previous, generation. I have been the recipient in this fashion of a computer desk, hard-drive, flat-screen monitor, vacuum cleaner, microwave, chest of drawers, and rather glorious desk chair. At first I was startled by the unexpected origin of these gifts. But I'm beginning to take it for granted that I will be not only offered, but taught by example (and sometimes by exhortation) many things by a generation whose capacities and capabilities I feel only fitfully responsible for. Although, when they are small, we can watch over the breath and sleep of those for whom we felt such duty of care, witnessing them as adults exceed us, in conscience and soul, in every way gives much more pleasure than its accompanying pain.

"The New House" will be appearing in *All Souls'*, my seventh collection of poetry, which Véhicule Press will be issuing in September 2012.

Bio:

Rhea Tregebov is the author of poetry, fiction and children's picture books. She has also edited a number of anthologies. She is Associate Professor of Creative Writing at the University of British Columbia, Vancouver, Canada, where she teaches poetry, children's literature and

Notes & Bios

literary translation. Her work has received a number of literary awards, including the J. I. Segal Award for fiction, the Pat Lowther Award, the Prairie Schooner Readers' Choice Award, and the Malahat Review Long Poem Award.

TROTTER, JOSHUA
"Leitmotiv"

"A noisy monument to a moment of silence."

Bio:

Joshua Trotter lives in Montreal. His first book, *All This Could Be Yours,* was published by Biblioasis in 2011.

WELLS, ZACHARIAH
"One and One"

I wrote this poem on an Acadian Lines bus to Fredericton, NB, somewhere between Halifax and Truro, NS, on November 3, 2010. I wrote it quickly—there's only an hour between the two cities—and have changed very little since. That's about all I can say for sure about the origins of "One and One." I don't know where it came from—besides the rather obvious, if deceptively complicated, answer "my mind"—and I am by no means sure what it signifies, though it may well have been influenced in part by my reading of neuroscientist Antonio Damasio's book on self-consciousness *Self Comes to Mind: Constructing the Conscious Brain.*

The only edit I made after drafting the poem was the addition of the tag line "after George Herbert." This, like so many things in poems, is both true and false. It's true insofar as it was written nearly 400 years after Herbert penned "Clasping of Hands," the poem I had in mind when I wrote the tag line. It's false, however, because I hadn't read Herbert's poem prior to composing my own—at least not so far as I can recall, but when you forget as much as I do, anything's possible. Serendipitously, I read "Clasping of Hands" several weeks after the bus trip that birthed "One and One," and I was bowled over by the kinship of syntax and rhetoric in the two poems. I thought it fitting, once they clasped hands in my mind, to wire them "implacably together."

Bio:

Originally from PEI, Zachariah Wells (www.zachariahwells.com) writes and edits in Halifax. His most recent collection is *Track & Trace.*

WILLIAMS, IAN
"Missed Connections: Walmart automotive dept—w4m"

The style of "Missed connections: Walmart automotive dept—w4m" shares thematic concerns with my other work. The speaker's attempt to make a human connection in an increasingly alien and technological social landscape is both amusing and distressing. Her loneliness is mediated by the very technology that separates her from other humans.

The poem also appears in my latest poetry collection, *Personals*

Bio:

Ian Williams is the author of *You Know Who You Are* (poems, Wolsak and Wynn, 2010), *Not Anyone's Anything* (stories, Freehand, 2011) and *Personals* (poems, Freehand, 2012).

Notes & Bios

He is the winner of the 2011 Danuta Gleed Literary Award for the best first English-language collection of short fiction and a finalist for the ReLit Prize for poetry. In 2012, CBC named Williams to its list of 10 Canadian Writers to Watch. Williams has held fellowships or residencies from Vermont Studio Center, Cave Canem, Kimmel Harding Nelson Center for the Arts, and Palazzo Rinaldi in Italy. His writing has appeared in *Fiddlehead, Arc, Contemporary Verse 2, Rattle, jubilat, Confrontation, Antigonish Review, Descant,* and *Matrix Magazine.* He holds a Ph.D. in English from the University of Toronto and is currently an English professor. His website is www.ianwilliams.ca.

YOUNG, PATRICIA

"A Crow`s Life"

"A Crow's Life" is one in a series of poems that explore the mating habits of animals and birds and insects. Like many of the poems in the series, this one assumes the voice of a creature.

The poem will be published in a collection with Palimpsest Books.

Bio:

Patricia Young is the author of eleven books of poetry and one of short fiction. She lives in Victoria, B.C.

YUAN, CHANGMING

"Awaiting"

Bio:

Changming Yuan, four-time Pushcart nominee, grew up in a remote Chinese village and authored several monographs before moving to Canada as an international student. With a PhD in English from the University of Saskatchewan, Changming teaches independently in Vancouver, where he lives with his wife and teenage son Allen Qing Yuan (who has published dozens of poems worldwide). Since mid-2005, Changming's poetry has appeared in nearly 540 literary journals/anthologies across 22 countries, which include *Asia Literary Review, The Best Canadian Poetry* (2009), *BestNewPoemsOnline, Exquisite Corpse, London Magazine, Paris/Atlantic, Poetry Kanto, SAND* and *Taj Mahal Review.* Although he has participated in few writing contests and won no poetry awards, he keeps hoping to find a Canadian publisher for his collection(s).

Long List

Adams, Rose.   "Geraniums"   *Grain,* Winter 2011
Babstock, Ken.   "Fending Off the Conservatism ..."   *Brick,* 87
Beaulieu, Derek.   "Rectangle Four"   *Canadian Literature*
Borson, Roo.   "Ossian's Folly..."   *Walrus, Oct* 2011
Cabri, Louis.   "Expression Factory"   *Windsor Review,* Fall 2011
Conn, Jan.   "Unquantifiable"   *LRC,* March 2011
Crummey, Michael.   "Boys"   *Mahalat,* 177
Davidson, Heather.   "Stroke"   *LRC,* Oct 2011
Dempster, Barry.   "Puddles"   *Dalhouse Review,* Spring 2011
Eckerlin, Jesse.   "How to Repossess a House"   *Encore,* Dec 8, 2011
Ferguson, Jesse Patrick.   "Beyond Red"   *Antigonish,* 165 Spring 2011
Guthrie, Hamish.   "Bottles"   *Queen's Quarterly,* Summer 2011
Guri, Helen.   "Model"   *(Hobo 13, poetry folio)*
Hancock, Brecken.   "Duos"   *Grain* 39.1, Fall 2011
Harvor, Elisabeth.   "By Noon What's Delirious"   *Ottawater,* issue 7
Heighton, Steven.   "World Enough"   *Arc* 65, Winter 2011
Heroux, Jason.   "Warning"   *ELQ* 35.1
Hofmann, Karen.   "Flickers"   *Malahat,* Spring 2011
Howell, Bill.   "Al Purdy's "Red Fox on Highway 500"   *Naa.. Review*
Jacob, Danny.   "Lawn Boy"   *Malahat,* 176
Jollimore, Troy.   "Charlie Brown"   *Walrus,* December 2011
Kerkhoven, John.   "Out of Place"   *Vallum,* Fall 2011
Knight, Erin.   "A Substitute for Everything"   *Quarc,* Issue 66
MacPherson, Jay.   "Plants"   *Descant,* 153
McCann, Marcus.   "Compiling, Collating"   *Ottawater,* issue 7
McGiffin, Emily.   "Fall"   *TNQ,* Fall 2011
Millar, Jay.   "More Trouble With The Obvious"   *This,* Jan 2011
Neilson, Shane.   "The Perfect Fatherhood"   *Fiddlehead,* Autumn 2011
Poile, Craig.   "Consumation"   *Fiddlehead,* 247
Powell, Kerry-Lee.   "The Lifeboat"   *The New Quarterly*
Richardson, Peter.   "August Scene at Spyros..."   *Arc* 65, Winter 2011
Riopelle, Shawn.   "Yellow Bird"   *Prairie Fire,* vol 23 no. 1
Rogers, Damian.   "From the Windows the Alley"   *TRB,* Sept 20 2011
Rose, Rachel.   "What We Heard About the Sea"   *CV2,* Winter 2011
Seymour, David.   "City Living"   *Event* 39.3
Sherman, Ken.   "Heart"   *ELQ* 35.1
Shonmaier, Eleonore.   "Men"   *Antigonish,* 167
Sol, Adam.   "Yellow House Spide"   *Event* 40.3
Surani, Moez.   "Everyday (Narration..."   *Grain,* Summer 2011
Taylor, Peter.   "Leitmotif"   *CV2,* Spring 2011
Thran, Nick.   "Dopamine"   *Walrus,* May 2011
Tierney, Matthew.   "Growth Food, (Hobo 13, poetry folio)"   *Walrus,* May 2011

Warner, Patrick.   "The Animal's Absolution"   *Riddle Fence #7*
Warrener, Sheryda.   "Recarnation Study…"   *Prism*, Summer 2011
Whetter, Darryl.   "The Softer Fossils…"   *Fiddlehead*, Spring 2011
Wingate, Shoshanna.   "Spring"   *Fiddlehead*, Spring 2011
Wolff, Elana.   "Into it"   *CV2*, Autumn 2011
Woodcock, Patrick.   "The Sandstorm"   *LRC*, December 2011
Rachel Zolf.   "Poem 39—A Tongue Listens to War"   *CV2*, Summer, 2011
Zomparelli, Daniel.   "Vancouver, After the Rain"   *CV2*, Winter 2011

Permissions

Permissions

Permissions

Magazines Considered For The 2012 Edition

The Antigonish Review
PO Box 5000
Antigonish, NS B2G 2W5
Tel: (902) 867-3962
Fax: (902) 867-5563
tar@stfx.ca
http://www.antigonishreview.com/

Arc: Canada's National Poetry
Magazine
PO Box 81060
Ottawa, ON K1P 1B1
http://www.arcpoetry.ca/

Branch Magazine
BranchMagazine.com
hello@branchmagazine.com
Gillian Sze, Editor

Brick: A Literary Journal
Box 609, Stn. P
Toronto, ON M5S 2Y4
http://www.brickmag.com/

Canadian Literature
University of British Columbia
1866 Main Mall-E 158
Vancouver, BC V6Y 1Z1
Tel: (604) 822-2780
Fax: (604) 822-5504
can.lit@ubc.ca
http://www.canlit.ca/

Canadian Notes & Queries
PO Box 92
Emerville, ON N0R 1A0
Tel: (519) 968-2206
Fax: (519) 250-5713
info@notesandqueries.ca
http://www.notesandqueries.ca/

Contemporary Verse 2: The
Canadian Journal of Poetry and
Critical Writing
207-100 Arthur St.

Winnipeg, MB R3B 1H3
Tel: (204) 949-1365
Fax: (204) 942-5754
cv2@mts.net
http://www.contemporaryverse2.ca/

Dalhousie Review
Dalhousie University
Halifax, NS B3H 4R2
Tel: (902) 494-2541
Fax: (902) 494-3561
dalhousie.review@dal.ca
http://dalhousiereview.dal.ca/

dANDelion Magazine
Department of English
The University of Calgary
2500 University Dr. N.W.
Calgary, AB T2N 1N4
http://www.dandelionmag.ca/

Descant
PO Box 314, Stn. P
Toronto, ON M5S 2S8
info@descant.ca
http://www.descant.ca/

ditch
http://ditchpoetry.com

Eighteen Bridges
Canadian Literature Centre
4-115 Humanities Centre,
University of Alberta
Edmonton, AB
T6G 2E5

enRoute Magazine
Spafax Canada
4200 boul. St-Laurent, Ste. 707
Montreal, QC H2W 2R2
Tel: (514) 844-2001
Fax: (514) 844-6001
http://enroute.aircanada.com/

116

Event
PO Box 2503
New Westminster, BC V3L 5B2
Tel: (604) 527-5293
Fax: (604) 527-5095
event@douglas.bc.ca
http://event.douglas.bc.ca/

Exile Quarterly
Exile/Excelsior Publishing Inc.
134 Eastbourne Ave.
Toronto, ON M5P 2G6
http://www.exilequarterly.com/
quarterly/

Existere: Journal of Arts and
Literature
Vanier College 101E
York University
4700 Keele Street
Toronto, ON M3J 1P3
existere.journal@gmail.com
http://www.yorku.ca/existere/

The Fiddlehead
Campus House
11 Garland Court
University of New Brunswick
PO. Box 4400
Fredericton, NB E3B 5A3
Tel: (506) 453-3501
Fax: (506) 453-5069
fiddlehd@unb.ca
http://www.thefiddlehead.ca/

Filling Station
PO. Box 22135, Bankers Hall
Calgary, AB T2P 4J5
http://www.fillingstation.ca/

Geist
341 Water Street, #200
Vancouver, BC V6B 1B8
http://www.geist.com/

Grain Magazine
PO Box 67
Saskatoon, SK S7K 3K1
Tel: (306) 244-2828
Fax: (306) 244-0255
grainmag@sasktel.net
http://www.grainmagazine.ca/

The Leaf
The Brucedale Press
Box 2259
Port Elgin, ON, N0H 2C0

Literary Review of Canada
581 Markham Street, Suite 3A
Toronto, ON M6G 2L7
review@lrcreview.com
http://reviewcanada.ca

Maisonneuve Magazine
4413 Harvard Ave.
Montreal, QC H4A 2W9
(514) 482-5089
submissions@maisonneuve.org
http://www.maisonneuve.org/

The Malahat Review
University of Victoria
PO. Box 1700, Station CSC
Victoria, BC V8W 2Y2
Tel: (250) 721-8524
Fax: (250) 472-5051
malahat@uvic.ca
http://malahatreview.ca

Maple Tree Literary Supplement (Mtls)
1103-1701 Kilborn Avenue
Ottawa ON K1H 6M8
P: (613) 355-6195
managingeditor@mtls.ca
http://www.mtls.ca

Matrix Magazine
1400 de Maisonneuve W.
Ste. LB-658

Montreal, QC H3G 1M8
info@matrixmagazine.org
http://www.matrixmagazine.org/

The Nashwaak Review
St. Thomas University
Fredericton, NB E3B 5G3
Tel: (506) 452-0426
Fax: (506) 450-9615
tnr@stu.ca
http://w3.stu.ca/stu/about/
publications/nashwaak/nashwaak.
aspx

The New Quarterly
St. Jerome's University
290 Westmount Rd. N.
Waterloo, ON N2L 3G3
editor@tnq.ca
http://www.tnq.ca/

Numero Cinq
http://numerocinqmagazine.com
Douglas Glover, Editor

The Ottawater
http://www.ottawater.com

Our Times
#407-15 Gervais Drive
Toronto, ON M3C 1Y8
Tel: (416) 703-7661
Toll-free: 1-800-648-6131
Fax: (416) 703-9094
office@ourtimes.ca
http://www.ourtimes.ca/index.php

Pacific Rim Review of Books
Box 8474 Main Postal Outlet
Victoria, BC V8W 3S1
Tel/Fax: (250) 385-3378
editor@prrb.ca
http://www.prrb.ca/index.html

Poetry Quebec
800 rue Gordon
Suite 205
Verdun, Quebec
H4G 2R9
poetry-quebec.com

poetry'zown
http://www.inkbottlepress.com/
POW/pow_open.htm

Prairie Fire
Prairie Fire Press, Inc.
423-100 Arthur St.
Winnipeg, MB R3B 1H3
Tel: (204) 943-9066
Fax: (204) 942-1555
prfire@mts.net
http://www.prairiefire.ca/about.
html

PRECIPICe
Department of English Language &
Literature
Brock University
500 Glenridge Ave.
St. Catharines, ON L2S 3A1
precipice@BrockU.CA
http://www.brocku.ca/precipice/

PRISM International
Creative Writing Program
University of British Columbia
Buchanan E462-1866 Main Mall
Vancouver, BC V6T 1Z1
Tel: (604) 822-2514
Fax: (604) 822-3616
http://prism.arts.ubc.ca/

Queen's Quarterly
Queen's University
144 Barrie St.
Kingston, ON K7L 3N6
Tel: (613) 533-2667
Fax: (613) 533-6822

queens.quarterly@queensu.ca
http://www.queensu.ca/quarterly

Rampike
English Department
University of Windsor
401 Sunset Ave.
Windsor, ON N9B 3P4
http://web4.uwindsor.ca/rampike

Rhythm
http://rhythmpoetrymagazine.
english.dal.ca/

Riddle Fence
PO Box 7092
St. John's, NL A1E 3Y3
(709) 739-6484
info@riddlefence.com
http://riddlefence.com/

Room
PO Box 46160, Stn. D
Vancouver, BC V6J 5G5
contactus@roommagazine.com
http://www.roommagazine.com/

Studio
http://www.ccfi.educ.ubc.ca/
publication/studio/index.html

subTERRAIN Magazine
PO Box 3008, MPO
Vancouver, BC V6B 3X5
Tel: (604) 876-8710
Fax: (604) 879-2667
subter@portal.ca
http://www.subterrain.ca/

Taddle Creek
PO Box 611, Stn. P
Toronto, ON M5S 2Y4
editor@taddlecreekmag.com
http://www.taddlecreekmag.com/

THIS Magazine
401 Richmond St. W., #396
Toronto, ON M5V 3A8
Editorial Tel: (416) 979-8400
Business Tel: (416) 979-9429
Fax: (416) 979-1143
info@thismagazine.ca
http://www.thismagazine.ca/

The Toronto Quarterly
http://thetorontoquarterly.blogspot.
com/

Vallum
PO Box 326, Westmount Stn.
Montreal, QC H3Z 2T5
Tel/Fax: (514) 237-8946
http://www.vallummag.com/

The Walrus
19 Duncan St., Ste. 101
Toronto, ON M5H 3H1
Tel: (416) 971-5004
Fax: (416) 971-8768
info@walrusmagazine.com
http://www.walrusmagazine.com/

West Coast LINE
2027 East Annex
8888 University Drive
Simon Fraser University
Burnaby, BC V5A 1S6
Tel: (604) 291-4287
Fax: (604) 291-4622
wcl@sfu.ca
http://www.westcoastline.ca/

The Winnipeg Free Press
editor@thewinnipegreview.com.
345-955 Portage Avenue
Winnipeg, MB R3G 0P9
thewinnipegreview.coms

CARMINE STARNINO

Carmine Starnino has published four critically acclaimed volumes of poetry, including *This Way Out* (2009), which was nominated for the Governor General's Award. His most recent book is *Lazy Bastardism: Essays and Reviews on Contemporary Poetry* (2012). Starnino lives in Montreal, where he is poetry editor for Vehicule Press and a senior editor for Reader's Digest Canada.

MOLLY PEACOCK

Her nonfiction includes The Paper Garden: Mrs. Delany Begins Her Life's Work at 72 and Paradise, Piece by Piece, a memoir, both published by McClelland and Stewart. Other essays and articles have been published in The Globe and Mail, MORE, O, the Oprah Magazine, Elle, House & Garden, and New York Magazine. She is also the editor of a collection of creative non-fiction, The Private I: Privacy in a Public World (Graywolf Press). Internationally published poet, essayist, and creative nonfiction writer Molly Peacock has been the Series Editor for *Best Canadian Poetry in English* since its inauguration in 2007. Author of six books of poetry, including *The Second Blush* (McClelland and Stewart) and *Cornucopia: New and Selected Poems*, her poems appear in leading literary journals in North America and the UK. Widely anthologized in textbooks as well as in *The Oxford Book of American Poetry* and *The Best of the Best American Poetry*, Peacock is also the author of *How To Read A Poem and Start A Poetry Circle* and the co-editor of *Poetry in Motion: One Hundred Poems from the Subways and Buses*. She is as well a Contributing Editor for the *Literary Review of Canada*.